SIMPLY SENSATIONAL
SCRAPBOOK CARDS

SIMPLY SENSATIONAL
SCRAPBOOK CARDS

Sue Nicholson

David and Charles

To my husband Ian, son Joshua, daughter Sarah and my brothers Christopher and Paul.

A DAVID & CHARLES BOOK
Copyright © David & Charles Limited 2006

David & Charles is an F+W Publications Inc. company
4700 East Galbraith Road
Cincinnati, OH 45236

First published in the UK in 2006

Text and project designs copyright © Sue Nicholson 2006

A catalogue record for this book is available from the British Library.

ISBN-13: 978-0-7153-2446-2 hardback
ISBN-10: 0-7153-2446-2 hardback

ISBN-13: 978-0-7153-2255-0 paperback
ISBN-10: 0-7153-2255-9 paperback

Printed in China by RRD
for David & Charles
Brunel House   Newton Abbot   Devon

Executive Editor Cheryl Brown
Editor Jennifer Proverbs
Art Editor Prudence Rogers
Designer Sarah Clark
Production Controller Ros Napper
Project Editor Betsy Hosegood

Visit our website at www.davidandcharles.co.uk

David & Charles books are available from all good bookshops; alternatively you can contact our Orderline on
0870 9908222 or write to us at FREEPOST EX2 110, D&C Direct, Newton Abbot, TQ12 4ZZ (no stamp required
UK only); US customers call 800-289-0963 and Canadian customers call 800-840-5220.

contents

introduction

Are you keen to use your photographs in imaginative and creative ways? Perhaps you have a stash of photos that you wish to share, or maybe you are a scrapbooker or card maker who wants to experiment with something new. If this sounds like you then within the pages of this book you'll find cards, albums, tips and ideas to inspire you and help you on your way.

In the first section I have concentrated on the materials that you will need for the projects in this book, passed on lots of tips and ideas and included ways to help you save both time and money. There is something there for everyone, irrespective of your card-making or scrapbooking experience.

The nine chapters that follow lead you through a variety of construction methods and styles for your cards. Starting off with the traditional tall card, (see page 26), I take you through designs that include an unusual long card (see page 38), cards with folds and pockets (see pages 44 and 50), and front-opening cards (see pages 56 and 62) concluding with a fantastic zigzag card (see page 74).

Building on these ideas but still keeping to a smaller scale you will find three very different mini scrapbook albums for you try. There is an unusual hanging album (see page 80), a traditional-style version with a popular binding system (see page 86) and a simple accordion-style album (see page 92).

As my cards and albums are of various dimensions I haven't forgotten that you will also need envelopes. Instead of the traditional flap style I have included a simple wrap design (see page 98) alongside an alternative idea based on the construction of a coin envelope (see page 100).

And for those bulky cards and albums that need more protection I have included instructions on how to create a presentation box (see page 102).

Illustrated step-by-step instructions enable you to complete each main card, album, envelope or box. Each chapter contains plenty of tips and suggestions and is supported with further variations. I am very aware that your photos and materials will be different to mine and therefore alongside each variation I have given you the reasons for my design considerations that led me to my final layout. This will help you to adapt my cards and albums so that they complement your own photos and selection of materials.

You may also want to translate some of the card designs into scrapbook pages. To show how simple this process is I have taken two very different cards and created scrapbook pages using the same ideas and materials (see page 104). Finally, continuing with 12 x 12in pages, there are ten ideas for scrapbook layouts that you can adapt and develop (see page 106).

I have thoroughly enjoyed putting together the ideas in this book and hope that they inspire you. I'd love to know how you get on and if you'd like to share your creation with me then please send me a photo (see page 111).

Happy crafting.

Love, peace, joy & happiness

Sue Nicholson

www.suenicholson.com

techniques

This chapter covers the basic tools and techniques required for the projects in this book, including information on the best tools and materials for the job. Find out how to crop photos and their mats and how to journal effectively. Learn the best way to centre text and images and discover a fail-safe way of attaching your photos to the card. Finally pick up some pointers on making inserts and tags.

Card maker's tool kit

Before you can begin making cards you need to collect the tools for the job. This tool kit contains a good selection to cover you needs for all types of card, and will help you complete the projects in this book.

Acid tester pen: use this to check card and paper that is not sold as acid free.

Acid-free adhesive: you have several options here. I would recommend the Studio Tac 'dry' glue in either tape or as a sheet, which is quick and easy to apply; Xyron machines, which can be used to apply adhesive to large or small areas, and Zig 2-way glue, which gives either a permanent or temporary bond.

Cocktail sticks: for picking up and spreading small amounts of glue or for picking up seed beads.

Bone folder: essential to give clean, sharp creases in card and paper (or use a clean, blunt knife).

Craft knife: always use a craft knife with a sharp blade to produce a crisp cut.

Bradawl: for making guide holes in card before using brads. It is available from hardware stores.

Cutting mat: self-healing cutting mats are ideal when using a craft knife because they are smooth and flat. They prolong the life of the knife and are easier to cut on than other surfaces.

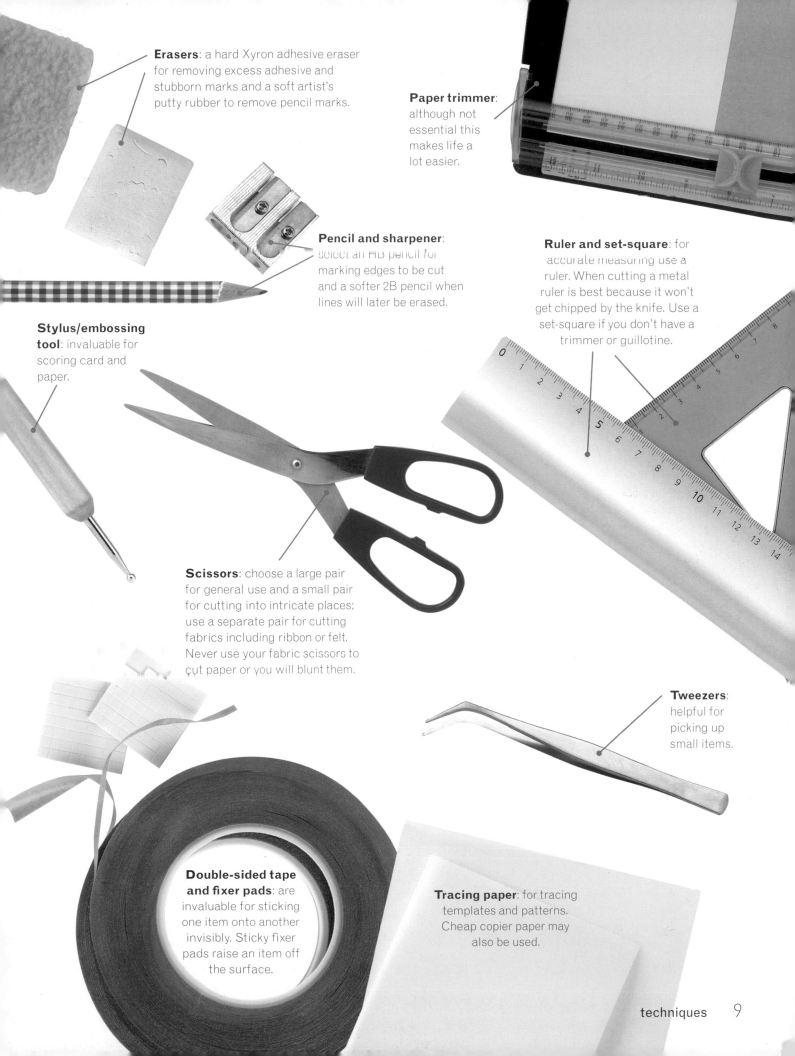

Erasers: a hard Xyron adhesive eraser for removing excess adhesive and stubborn marks and a soft artist's putty rubber to remove pencil marks.

Paper trimmer: although not essential this makes life a lot easier.

Pencil and sharpener: select an HB pencil for marking edges to be cut and a softer 2B pencil when lines will later be erased.

Ruler and set-square: for accurate measuring use a ruler. When cutting a metal ruler is best because it won't get chipped by the knife. Use a set-square if you don't have a trimmer or guillotine.

Stylus/embossing tool: invaluable for scoring card and paper.

Scissors: choose a large pair for general use and a small pair for cutting into intricate places; use a separate pair for cutting fabrics including ribbon or felt. Never use your fabric scissors to cut paper or you will blunt them.

Tweezers: helpful for picking up small items.

Double-sided tape and fixer pads: are invaluable for sticking one item onto another invisibly. Sticky fixer pads raise an item off the surface.

Tracing paper: for tracing templates and patterns. Cheap copier paper may also be used.

protecting your creations

Inappropriate papers and glues can have a horrible effect on your photographs and paper mounts, leading to rapid fading and even staining or bleaching them. Use the following materials to maximize the life of your cards and help keep them in pristine condition.

Photo paper: I used matt 280gsm 100% acid-free photo paper by Fotospeed. I experimented with a mixed pack of papers and found that the matt photos were far more forgiving when handled and therefore ideal for my projects. To maintain continuity I used this paper throughout this book. I have since tried smooth, pearl and classic pearl by Ilford and these also give beautiful results. Don't skimp on photo paper – buy good quality and experiment with different textures and weights.

simply stylish

Many times the most impressive cards and scrapbook pages are the simplest. You do not have to re-create exactly the cards or layouts in this book but instead take just some of the elements and make your own scaled-down version.

Acid-free/photo-safe adhesives: always ensure that the adhesives you use are acid-free or photo-safe. These will not disintegrate over time or react with you photos and papers causing damage. There is a wide range of these glues available from craft shops (see page 8) so do not be tempted to use whatever you find in the cupboard!

Sheet protectors: these are clear acid-free page protectors that are available for manufactured albums. Scrapbook pages are stored in these to protect against fingerprints, dust and other materials. For the cards and albums in this book I suggest making an envelope or presentation box from acid-free materials for protection.

Take a copy

I store my original photos and negatives and always use copies on my cards and in my albums. Firstly I size the photograph and print out two copies, one on inexpensive copier paper and the other on good-quality photo paper. I keep the good photo in a page protector near my work area so I can see the true colours but I work with the draft photo as I change and rearrange the layout. When I have done all that I can, only then do I secure my good photo in place.

Acid-free/lignin-free paper and card: papers and card that are suitable for archival use are normally labelled as acid-free and/or lignin-free. This describes the qualities ideal for scrapbooking. Initially you may wish to purchase your paper from a specialist scrapbooking store that supplies only appropriate materials, but as you gain experience you may want to source your paper and card from other places and at this point I suggest in investing in an acid tester pen.

Where pages touch, as in the albums or some of the cards, you will need to protect these pages so they don't cause indentations etc. Use acid-free paper, card or a cut down page protector as a removable sheet between the layers.

scoring and folding

Take a little time to understand card and how to fold it properly because a buckled fold can spoil even the most beautiful card. With a little practice you will soon be making your own card blanks, opening up further possibilities, saving money and enhancing your sense of achievement.

mountains and valleys

You may hear card manufacturers refer to mountain or valley folds. Quite simply in a mountain fold the bend of the fold points upwards and in a valley fold it points downwards, resembling a valley.

Selecting card

The ideal weight of your card is 240/280gsm. If the weight of the card is not given, hold the card in one hand and gently move it (just a little shake). The resistance that you feel should help you to decide whether it will be suitable, too flimsy to stand up or too heavy to fold.

Card grain

Like fabric, paper and card have a grain. The neatest folds run in the direction of the grain rather than across it. When a fold is made across the grain the top layer can split and look ragged, a particular problem with doubled-sided coloured card or card that has a special finish, such as a pearlized card. Ideally you should cut your card so that the fold will run along the grain. It would be helpful if the grain on A4 (US letter) card and paper always ran from top to bottom. Unfortunately this cannot be guaranteed and you will need to check the direction of the grain for yourself. To find the grain use one of the methods here.

Finding the grain

Partly fold the card first widthways and then lengthways without forming a crease, as shown here. Whichever bends more easily is the direction of the grain.

Alternatively, cut a small piece of the card and score and fold it from top to bottom and then from side to side. The fold made with the grain will be much neater than the one made across it.

Cutting card

A paper trimmer/guillotine provides the quickest and neatest means of cutting card accurately. This is a worthwhile investment if you are making all your own greetings cards. Alternatively, measure the card stock to the required dimensions and mark with pencil, using a set square to keep the corners true. Trim the card to size on the cutting mat using a craft knife and metal ruler. Ideally use one continuous cutting movement for each side that you cut.

Scoring card

Scoring card prior to folding breaks the surface fibres of the card, allowing it to be folded neatly and precisely. If you have a guillotine use a scoring blade or run a stylus (embossing tool) along the cutting guide. Alternatively, find the position of the fold with a ruler, use a set square to position it accurately and draw a stylus along the edge.

Folding card

Use a bone folder to smooth down the fold for a sharp and accurate crease.

photo styles

The kind of photo to use will be dictated by the type of layout, the design and subject matter as well as personal preference. I think that sometimes we are so used to seeing colour photos that we often forget the option of using traditional black-and-white or tinting to sepia and other colours.

Computers make it easy to adjust the look of a photograph, perhaps to give it an old-world or classical look, but even without one you'll find that many processing labs will print in different styles for you. The important thing is to be aware of your options and don't just go for the obvious. These are your basic choices:

Colour, which has a vibrancy about it and brings the image alive. It's as close to reality as you can get.

Black and white allows the true beauty to shine through without clouding the vision. It can create a sophisticated look, and because most photos are in colour these days, it will stand out from the crowd.

Black-and-white photos don't have to mean black-and-white cards. Add colour with the paper, as shown left.

Sepia ages an image and can be very flattering for portraits in particular.

Other tints can create a contemporary, eye-catching look – navy blue and most browns work particularly well.

Add continuity to a group of photos with clashing backgrounds by converting them all to black and white as I did for A Great Grandpa, page 54.

If you want to focus on the central image but keep the background in view a good idea is to secure a trimmed colour photo onto a second copy that has been tinted as in Across the Miles, left (see page 76).

This scrapbook (see page 86) uses a mixture of black-and-white and colour images from across the years. Not only is it authentic, but it visually emphasizes the passing of time for a nostalgic feel.

cropping and cutting mats

The photographs you pick up from the developing lab or that you download onto your computer can often be improved by cropping and can be made to stand out by layering them on one or more slightly larger pieces of card or paper. These are known as photo mats.

The most important element of your card is the photograph so consider if you can improve it by trimming off unwanted detail or by cutting it in an unusual shape. A photocopy or print-out on ordinary copier paper comes in handy here, as you can experiment on the cheap copy before taking a blade to the quality photo. Cropping can improve a picture beyond measure, and a mat will give it a professional look and draw the eye.

I used to find it almost impossible to position my card/photo centrally onto a pre-cut mat, so I played around with my paper trimmer and came up with the technique explained below. It works every time and saves me much measuring and fiddling about. I use a Fiskars paper trimmer so if you are using a different trimmer you may need to adapt the instructions to work with your model.

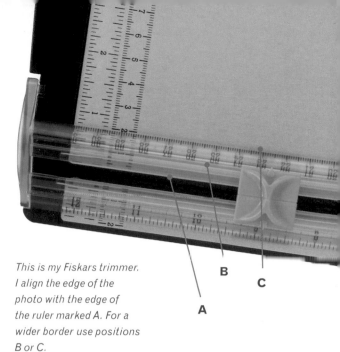

This is my Fiskars trimmer. I align the edge of the photo with the edge of the ruler marked A. For a wider border use positions B or C.

Cutting an even mat

1 Cut your mat 2cm (¾in) wider and deeper than the smaller mat/photo. Secure the smaller mat/photo on the mat. Get it roughly central with the sides parallel but don't spend time doing this precisely.

2 Place your mat into your paper trimmer and align one edge of the smaller mat/photo with the nearest edge in the slot for the blade (A); trim.

3 Butt the trimmed edge up to the side of the paper trimmer to achieve a true right angle cut and repeat step 2. Repeat twice more to create even borders all round.

Consider how the colour or pattern of the mat can complement the theme of the card. This spotty Christmas design is perfect for a festive photograph (see page 32).

journaling

As every scrapbooker will know, journaling is the text on your page that might describe the event pictured or proclaim the author's feelings about those featured. It is often written by hand as a personal touch. Everyone journals in a different way. Like lifestyle, what works for one person doesn't always work with someone else. So just as scrapbook layouts vary from person to person, the way we journal is also a matter of taste and, ultimately, time.

Something to think about…

Your scrapbook or card is a work of love to be cherished and treasured over the years to come. It will not be marked with a red pen and graded A, B, C or D! It is your creation to do with as you wish and in your own style. If you spend too much time worrying how to begin, you may find that you never get started at all, so bite the bullet and start moving. To help you with the process I have come up with a set of questions. Just relax and sit comfortably with your photo(s) in front of you. On a piece of paper write down the answers to some of the questions here. Note that not all questions will be relevant to every photograph or situation.

What

* *What is happening in the photo? Does it happen often or is it a one-off?*
* *Did you have a good time?*
* *What happened before it was taken? Did the scene need to be set or was it taken on the spur of the moment?*
* *What happened afterwards?*
* *What was the weather like? Is it obvious?*
* *What were the smells? A smoky barbecue, sweet bubble bath, rich chocolate?*
* *What makes this photo unusual, funny, sad or important?*
* *What words does it bring to mind? Can you remember the conversation or the music that was playing? Does it remind you of a song, a poem or quote?*
* *What else do you have that you can use to tell the story? Do you have tickets, pressed flowers, a lock of hair, a recipe or letter?*
* *What is it that you like about this particular photo? Write down five things about the main person or place.*

When

* *When was this photo taken? Try to recall the date and time or just state the occasion and year, such as Christmas Day 2000 or Halloween 2005.*
* *When are you creating your scrapbook card/page? Are you going to record your journaling date?*

Why

* *Why was the photo taken? Is it of a special birthday, wedding anniversary, the first day of spring, just for fun or to capture a fantastic view?*

Who

* *Who is in your photo? Name as much as possible, everyone and everything.*
* *Who isn't in it, and why are they missing? (For example, 'Jo was staying with friends that day'.)*
* *Who took this photo and why?*
* *Who else could have information about it? Can you get in touch with them?*
* *Who else have you shown the photo to, and what did they have to say about it?*

How

* *How does your photo make you feel? For example, happy, nostalgic, sad.*
* *How does it make others feel? Does it have the same effect on them?*
* *How did you come by the photo? Is it yours or were you given it?*
* *How are you going to journal this information? Think about the various styles such as story telling, a letter, short notes or bullet points.*

Finally

Now walk away from the photo and paper. Leave it an hour, or better still overnight, (I often find that sleep seems to bring back more memories without any extra effort!) Return to your notes then read through your questions and answers. Can you add anything else?

Where

* *Where was this photo taken? Is there any history about this place?*
* *Where were you at the time of the photo? Were you born, living in the same area or on the other side of the world?*

Writing it down

Now you are ready to create your journaling. So how are you going to do this? Here are just a few suggestions and don't forget you can mix and match different styles.

Pens: write in your own handwriting using an acid-free pen. I think that it is wonderful to come across hand written journaling so I always try to include some in mine. If you are unhappy about the style of your handwriting then hide it away in a pocket or under a flap.

Stamps: try some rubber stamping or heat embossing. There are lots of different effects that can be achieved to co-ordinate with your design. There are sayings, quotes and a wide range of alphabets that can be used effectively on both cards and scrapbook pages.

Typing: if you own a home computer then this will offer you infinite possibilities for journaling. With tools to spell check and a thesaurus to help express yourself more clearly you can type away to your heart's content. Add to this the vast number fonts and the ease with which a single line or a whole paragraph can be changed, and you can see why it is so popular.

Alphabets, brads, rub-ons, stickers: Alphabet embellishments, such as stickers, rub-ons and tiles are wonderful. They are ideal for adding impact but they can be time consuming to align so I suggest tilting the letters to create a wacky effect or limiting their use to a few sentences. They are also very effective when used to pick out important words within a written paragraph. In addition to alphabets there are also packs providing quotes and sayings.

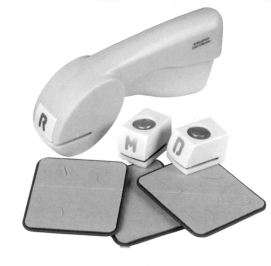

Punched letters: utilize leftover scraps of paper and card by either punching out your letters using a cassette craft punch or by using one of the many die-cutting alphabets.

Dynamo: use a label maker to create labels or embossed stickers. The LetraTag prints onto paper, plastic, metallic and fabric tapes, while the traditional Dynamo Junior will produce raised embossed text on coloured or metallic tapes.

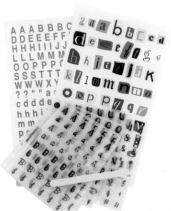

Voice pad: you can incorporate a voice pad or cassette recordings to add that extra special message.

cutting your own letters

If you have a computer with software capable of producing a mirror image, which many word-processing and creative packages can do, then you can print out the letters that you want on the reverse of your paper or card and cut them out for use on your layouts. Here's how.

See also:
Paper Saving,
page 17

no computer?

Flip over an alphabet stencil and use a pencil to transfer the letters directly onto the back of your card or paper. Alternatively write the letters freehand on copier paper, cut out, flip over and trace onto your card or paper.

Printing the letters

1

2

Type in the text and alter the font and size of each letter to suit your needs. Print onto copier paper, adjust as necessary then create a mirror image. Print the mirror image onto the wrong side of your card or paper. Cut roughly round the letters and lay each one onto the copier paper. Using fine pointed scissors or a craft knife, trim each letter to shape. You do not need to remove all the printed lines of the letter as it is on the underside and won't be seen when the letter is glued in place.

When cutting into a V-shaped area you may find that you need to pull the excess card away from the letter. Do this by pulling it down the wrong side of the letter so that if the top layer of card tears the right side of the letter will remain intact.

letter guide

Only use the printed letters as a guide. When the letters are cut out and glued in place no one is going to say that you didn't take enough from the I and too much from the Y!

removing middles

Try using a hole punch to cut away the centre from the letter O or a small flower punch to create effective and unusual cut outs in the letter B.

On my SK8er Boy scrapbook page (see page 104) I used a simple method to create my own die-cut type of letters, as explained above. I used four different fonts in the title and each letter was one of three different sizes. This technique is very effective and has endless possibilities.

paper saving

Printing one photo in the middle of an expensive sheet of photo paper is not only wasteful but makes the photo very costly indeed. With my method of printing directly onto a smaller piece of photo paper you can virtually eliminate waste and get full value from your paper and card. I came up with this paper-saving solution many years ago and use it all the time. It also works with text, clip art and anything else that you want to print from your computer.

Printing on paper fragments

Draw an arrow on a sheet of inexpensive copier paper. Place it in the printing tray ensuring that the arrow is facing towards the printing mechanism then print the photo using draft quality to save on ink. Remove the copier paper from the printer. Cut a piece of photo paper to roughly 1cm (¼in) longer and wider than the printed image and cover the image with it. Refer to the arrow to determine which edge will go back into the printer first and secure the photo paper to the copier paper along this edge with a little masking tape.

Place the paper back in the printing tray, once again with the arrow facing towards the printing mechanism. Change the printer settings to photo quality and print the image again. The image is now on the photo paper. Because it has been printed so that the edges are parallel to the copier paper and not the photo paper it is easier to trim your image with a paper trimmer while it is still secured to the paper.

The paper-saving method also works for printing journaling and lettering, as on this bon voyage card, featured on page 43.

the right side

Most photo papers have a right side for printing on so when selecting a new sheet from the pack lightly scribble on the wrong side with pencil. Now when cutting pieces from it you will be able to identify the right side immediately.

which tape?

It is unlikely that ink will inadvertently get onto the tape holding the photo paper in place but I use DIY masking tape so that if it should happen the ink will be absorbed. Alternatively you can secure the photo paper using narrow width double-sided tape. Personally I would avoid shiny sticky tape because the ink will sit on top and could smear.

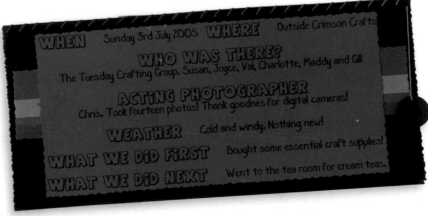

Creating an even border around text or an image can prove challenging. I
devised two methods to centre text or an image with, or without, a computer.

With a computer

1

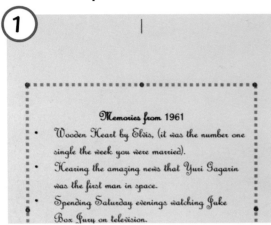

2

Type in the text and highlight it on the screen so
that you can see the text box border with four
corner points and four centre points. Create a mid
point guideline by using the line command to draw
a small vertical line above the text. This should be
aligned with the top centre point and far enough
away not to be caught within the border. Print out.

To find the cutting lines for the left and right edges
halve the desired overall width. With a ruler make
this measurement out from the mid point on each
side and mark the paper with a pencil to show the
cutting lines.

top to bottom

To use the computer
method to centre text
within a given depth draw
a mid point guideline that
is aligned with one of
the side centre points on
the text box. When using
the freehand method
just repeat the same
steps as before but this
time mark the top edge
of the paper strip and
keep it aligned with the
top edge of the paper.

Without a computer

1

2

Cut a strip of paper to the width of the paper with
the text. Identify its left-hand side by writing 'L' on
the strip. Now use a pencil to mark the strip where
the furthest left piece of text begins and where the
furthest right piece of text ends. You may need to
move the strip up and down the page but always
keep the left edges together.

Fold the strip in half so that the two marks meet,
crease well, open up and mark the fold. To find
the cutting lines for the left and right edges halve
the desired overall width. With a ruler make this
measurement out from the fold on each side and
mark the strip with a pencil. Replace the strip,
once again lining up the left-hand edges, and
transfer the cutting marks onto the paper.

centring die-cuts

I often use craft punches upside down to enable me to centre a pattern or text within the shape before punching out (see New Birth on page 30). I wanted to be able to do the same with my dies but these are completely different in construction so I played around with a couple of methods and came up with the idea of using a card template. This is easy and very effective.

(see New Birth on page 30)

(see page 56).

Die-cutting

1

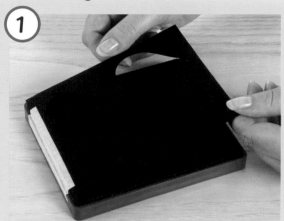

Cut a piece of scrap card to the size of your die and secure it to one end with masking tape. Die-cut the card and remove and discard the cut shapes. Leave the template secured in place.

2

Slide the patterned paper or text between the die and the template and move it around until it is centred within the shape. Hold the template firmly against the die, turn over and cut.

3

Lift the template to remove the die-cut paper shape, as shown.

✳ trusty template

The template can remain in position while making ordinary die-cuts in the usual way so once created the template can be used time and time again.

✳ other die-cuts

This technique is shown with Sizzix dies but it is adaptable to the other systems.

✳ is it secure?

If you think that you paper will move as you turn the die over then use a small piece of tape to hold it securely.

The versatile template allowed me to create a perfect selection of differently sized hearts cut from patterned paper (see page 56).

securing paper and photos

Everyone has their favourite technique for securing paper and photos in place and this is mine. I use it time and time again with brilliant results.

Using double-sided tape

①

②

Add 2mm ($\frac{1}{16}$in) to the width of your double-sided tape. On the back of your paper measure down this amount along the left-hand edge and make a mark with a pencil. Line up the double-sided tape with this mark, stick it down to the bottom edge, cut and press into place.

Turn the paper clockwise so that the tape now runs across the top. Secure the next piece of tape down the left-hand edge starting just below the previous tape, stick it down to the bottom edge, cut and press into place. Repeat twice more. From the corner end of each strip peel back a little of the backing paper, fold outwards and crease.

③

④

Turn the paper over and lay it onto the card, lining it up by eye or with pencil guidelines. As there is only a little sticky tape exposed you will be able to lift and move it around until you are happy with the position. Only then firmly press each corner to hold down the paper.

Use one hand to hold the paper in place. Use the other to remove one of the backing papers by pulling the folded backing paper outwards. Press firmly and repeat with the remaining tapes.

small shapes

Not all papers need to be secured along all edges. When working with small shapes you may find that tape along two edges is sufficient to hold the paper securely.

long edges

when working with really long edges, secure one piece of tape to the approximate halfway point and cut. Secure a second piece from this point to the end. In step 2 also fold back the ends of tape at the halfway points.

terrific tags

A tag is just like a parcel label. It can hang free to provide movement or you can tuck it in a pocket or favour bag or stick it in place. It's a good way of drawing attention to a photo, words or messages, or alternatively of slipping them out of sight. Most tags have a hole punched in the top or sides that enable you to make use of fibres and ribbons, but you can omit the holes if desired.

You can buy tags for your cards, often as part of a variety pack, or you can make them yourself. There are several die-cuts available if you wish, or you can make simple tags by cutting basic rectangles or squares out of card. Punch a hole in the tag if desired.

Sometimes there are lots of things that you want to say, but not enough room on the card for words and images. In Joshua's birthday card (see page 61), I got around this problem by making journal-led tags, which I popped into pockets behind the photos.

This card uses a tag in the most popular way. The tag conveys a greeting and is particularly appropriate for a Christmas card because it reminds us of all those lovely gift labels. (This delightful Christmas card is shown on page 60.)

Here a large tag is used to display a poem and greeting. This would take up too much of the card if left on display, but it is an important element of the card so it is stored in a pocket on the card back. (For further details, see page 67.)

Home is where you can be silent
and still be heard...

Where you can ask
and find out who you are...

Where people laugh with you
about yourself...

Where sorrow is divided
and joy multiplied...

Where we share and love and grow.
Anon.

To Jenny, Rob, Peter, Michael and Claire
Sending you our very best wishes
as you settle in to your new home.
Although no longer neighbours we will
cherish you as friends forever.

Love Linda, Steve, Charlotte & Christopher

Handmade especially for you on 15th July 2005

(Photo taken last week)

Stickers are ideal for decorating large areas of text, like the greeting on this Easter card. When the tag is in the pocket on the card back you can see some of the stickers as well as a pretty ribbon, which help to draw attention to the tag. (This Easter card is shown on page 42.)

A small favour bag makes an unusual holder for five seasonal message tags on this greetings card. The titles of the messages are created with stickers that echo the green and red colour theme of the card. (For further details, see page 73.)

making inserts

I am a great believer that adding an insert is the final touch that makes your card look professional. Without one a card can sometimes look exactly what it is – a piece of card folded in half! But by adding a complementary insert you can transform it from the ordinary to the extraordinary in one easy step.

mix and match

Inserts don't have to be white or cream. Try using paper in pastels or brights, papers with faint patterns and pretty vellums.

Die-cutting

1

Measure the width of the folded card and subtract 5mm (³⁄₁₆in) from it (W). Measure the height of the card and subtract 1cm (³⁄₈in) from it (H). Fold the insert paper in half and crease well. Measure out from the fold and trim to W then measure up the fold and trim to H.

2

Apply 3mm (¹⁄₈in) wide double-sided tape to the back of the folded insert along, but not over, the fold. Alternatively apply a thin line of glue. Open the card and, keeping the distance between the top and bottom edges of the card equal, butt the insert up to the card fold. Press in place.

you will need

✓ Card maker's tool kit, page 8
✓ Paper (see step 1 for amount)

See also
Scoring and folding, page 11

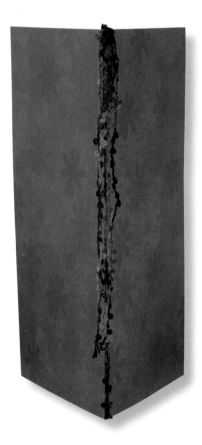

Instead of using glue or tape to secure a folded insert, you can use fibre, ribbons or thread very effectively, as shown above. Simply tie it round the card, knot and trim to length or punch holes in the spine of the card and the insert and then thread ribbon or cord through the holes.

pretty in pink

For more details on making this card, see page 37.

The insert (shown below) reflects the contemporary style of the card front and echoes its colours.

The insert doesn't need to repeat the motifs on the card and it can be much less elaborate, but it should reflect the card's overall style.

In keeping with the main colour theme, I printed this double-page insert in deep pink on pale pink paper.

The decorative pastel squares link the insert to the design on the card front.

Amy Lou
Harris
Born
7th October
2004
Christened
20th March
2005

Every child
born into the world is a
new thought
of God, an ever fresh and
radiant possibility.

Kate Douglas Wiggins

The left-hand side of the insert gives the details of Amy Lou's birth and christening.

I sourced an appropriate poem to express my sentiment. It is important to give credit to the author of the words you have chosen.

For a contemporary feel I used different sizes of one font. You could take this further by using two or three different fonts.

two for one

For more details on making this card, see page 37.

I printed two separate pages of text in dark grey on white paper because I found that the grey presented a softer, more pleasing effect than black.

The card shows around the insert and through the punched border for a truly co-ordinated effect.

The delicate corner design was created with a border punch. No measuring was involved – I simply lined up the end of the punch with the edge of the paper!

The left-hand insert includes memories from the year of the wedding. Try using old photos, letters and the Internet to jog your memory.

The front of the card uses the same simple colour scheme of pink, white and shades of grey.

Each insert was trimmed into a square a little smaller that the card and secured with double-sided tape.

Memories from 1961

- Wooden Heart by Elvis, (it was the number one single the week you were married).
- Hearing the amazing news that Yuri Gagarin was the first man in space.
- Spending Saturday evenings watching Juke Box Jury on television.
- The Duke of Kent marrying Katherine Worsley at York Minster and Petula Clark marryi-g Claude Wolf.
- Twisting all night to Chubby Checker.
- Breakfast at Tiffany's

With love and happiness
on your
45th
Wedding Anniversary

The greeting is printed on the right-hand insert.

in a flap

For more details on making this card, see page 36.

This card demanded an equally bold and dynamic insert.

I sourced a font that was appropriate for the card and printed it in large letters on the red card.

This insert is only attached to the card along the top, creating a flap that can be lifted to write a personal greeting underneath.

Eyelets secure the insert for a youthful, modern feel. These eyelets also feature on the front of the card.

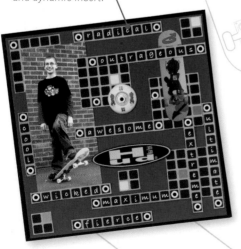

thanks for the present

tag it

For more details on making this card, see page 31.

As there are small tags on the card front I decided to keep with this theme, die-cutting the words into a large tag.

The tag is secured with a small green brad for added dimension and colour.

I broke the sentiment down into chunks for a modern feel then printed onto yellow card.

It usually works best if you use the same colours from the card front on the insert. In this case the paper used on the front is echoed inside by the red insert, yellow tag and green brad.

fine focus

For more details on making this card, see page 31.

Simplicity and a quality photo were the secret of this card's success, so I kept to the same lines on the insert.

To share your birthday joy with you,
I've made this cake with candle too.

I'll light it on your special day,
So we can share our love that way.

I choose a white paper insert in keeping with the colours and simple lines of this card.

For drama I cropped my original cake photo to leave only the candle in view and I positioned the photo on the insert using computer software.

The poem was printed in matching pink ink to maintain the two-colour scheme.

look who's 40

The standard, portrait format is the ideal way to begin making scrapbook cards. Just one simple image can make a striking impact and selecting a tall slim card blank will ensure that your design will stand out from all the rest on a celebration such as a milestone birthday, as here. For other ways in which this popular format can make a lasting impression, whatever the occasion, see pages 30–31.

The idea for the theme of this card came from the small advertisements often seen in the classified sections of local newspapers where baby photographs are used as illustrations to celebrate an adult's birthday. The original baby photographs were copied and used for the card so that the originals could be supplied separately as a gift. The subtle colour scheme of burgundy and silver complements the black and white photographs and helps to maintain the historical look, though sepia or faded blue would also work very well.

Parchlucent and leftover pieces of burgundy and silver card were used to make a co-ordinating vellum envelope that allows the recipient to get a glimpse of the card but not the greeting, which remains hidden behind the border until the card is removed. For full details on making this type of envelope see page 100.

variations on the theme

This card could be adapted in many different ways. You could turn it into a humorous party invitation for your own birthday, for example, and add a photo of yourself now beneath one of the tags. Why not try using old wedding photos to celebrate an important wedding anniversary?

Look who's 40

you will need

✓ Card maker's tool kit, page 8
✓ Black and white photos
   • 8.5cm (3¼in) square
   • 5cm (2in) square
✓ 10 x 20cm (4 x 8in) white textured card blank
✓ 8.5 x 9.5cm (3¼ x 3¾in) silver striped card
✓ Burgundy-brown card
   • 8.5 x 12.5cm (3½ x 4⅞in) rectangle
   • leftover piece
✓ 20cm (8in) of 2cm (¾in) wide white wired
   sheer ribbon
✓ 3cm (1¼in) diameter silver metal tag
✓ Small silver brad
✓ Circle punch with a 2.5cm (1in) diameter
✓ Use of a computer and printer or rubber
   stamps or rub-on letters

Card size 10 x 20cm (4 x 8in)

See also
Techniques,
pages 8–25
Materials,
page 110
Suppliers,
page 111

design decisions

Ribbon adds a soft, feminine touch and picks up the white of the photo and card blank. The wired edges on the ribbon help it keep its shape.

The large tag photo is matted at the top and bottom edges only for a trendy look and so it sits well on the tall card format.

The small round photo on the second tag adds further interest.

Look who's 40

---

tag hole template

To mark the position of the holes for the top tag accurately, first cut a strip of card 2 x 11cm (¾ x 4⅜in). Lay it on top of the card front and make a pencil mark where it crosses the left- and right-hand edges. Fold the strip in half so that the marks meet, crease well and open up. Make a mark 5mm (³⁄₁₆in) each side of the fold. Line up the edge of the template with the top edge of the card front and the card edges with the outer marks. Use the pencil to mark where the two 5mm (³⁄₁₆in) marks touch the card.

1

To make the tags, first measure from the centre top of the burgundy rectangle down by 5mm (³⁄₁₆in) and mark with the pencil. Place the hole punch over the mark and punch out a hole. Measure 1.5cm (⅝in) down from the top of the tag and draw a faint pencil guideline. Use double-sided tape to secure the silver card to the tag up to this line. Measure 5mm (³⁄₁₆in) down from the top of the silver card and draw a faint guideline. Glue the larger photo on top of the silver card up to this line.

2

Mark with the pencil where to make the hole for the circular tag on the card blank by measuring 5cm (2in) up from the bottom and 5cm (2in) across the card. Mark the holes for the main tag 2cm (¾in) down and 5mm (³⁄₁₆in) either side of the centre point using a template for accuracy (see the tip, left).

Thread one end of the ribbon from inside to outside through one of the top holes on the card blank. Feed the other end through the second hole and pull gently until the ends are even. Feed both ends through the single hole in burgundy card.

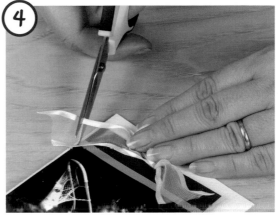

Gently pull each end of the ribbon outwards and move the tag towards the card. Adjust the tag position and use sharp scissors to trim the ribbon ends to the width of the tag and at a slant. The tag will still have a little movement so if you prefer it to be static then add a dab of glue underneath.

it's a tie

Using ribbon, string or thread to tie items onto a card works particularly well with transparent items such as vellum, when the glue may be seen, or plastic, when the glue may peel off when dry.

Turn the circular punch over, feed in the photo you are using for the small tag and adjust it so that the image is within the circle; punch out. Glue the circle onto the silver tag so that the bottom lines up with the bottom of the tag. Print out the greeting onto thin white card. Trim the text so that it has a small border then cut a mat from leftover burgundy card. Use double-sided tape to secure the text on the burgundy card and then to fix the text and mat to the card blank.

For the insert, first use computer software to import the same 5cm (2in) square photo image that you used to decorate the small metal circle. Position it to the far right of the page near the bottom. Type in the place information underneath and print out. To determine where to make the fold on the insert so that the photo is central make a paper template (see the tip, right).

Score and fold your insert then trim the width. The height of the insert is 19.5cm (7¾in), so decide how far down you want your photo and trim any excess from the bottom. Now trim the excess from the top. Ensure that your photo is on the inside of your insert then secure in place using double-sided tape that has been applied on the inside to the right of the fold.

insert template

Cut a strip of paper the width of the insert – 9.5cm (3¾in) – and find the mid-point by folding it in half; open up. Measure and mark half the width of the photo – 2.5cm (1in) – on each side of the fold. Line up the paper so that the photo is between the two 2.5cm (1in) marks then make a pencil mark where the edges of the template touch the insert. The left-hand mark is where to fold the insert and the right hand one is the cutting line.

The standard portrait card format is infinitely adaptable. It is useful when the photograph can be cropped in a tall format, as on the cake birthday card opposite. However, it also works well when you wish to use more than one image or a message.

Full details of the papers and embellishments used for the cards on these pages are provided on page 110.

new birth

Doubling as a keepsake, this card captures Leon James within a few hours of his birth. The vellum overlay, with its cutaway around the face, draws attention to the important area of the image.

Card size A5 (6 x 8¼in)

Although the focus of this photo is the baby, I kept the mother's arm and hands in the photo to provide perspective and to convey the warm welcome the baby received. To draw your eye to the baby, I used a cleverly cut vellum overlay.

Babies are often associated with frilly items so I added some detail to the heart with a small hole punch to create a lacy edge. It is secured on the left of the card to balance the aperture on the right.

The cotton tied through the buttons is a novel effect and adds dimension and texture. These buttons also cover up the glue dots that hold the vellum in place.

To focus attention on the baby, I blurred the background with a pale blue vellum overlay. I cut the aperture in the overlay using a square punch then placed the aperture over the baby's head and trimmed the vellum to the size of the photo.

Leon James
14th February
2003

birthday friendship

True friendship and the joy of giving are beautifully presented in this card. The two friends make a delightful image and the use of small gifts within the design ensures double the fun for the recipient.

Card size 14.5 x 20cm (5¾ x 8in)

The bracelet and charm can be removed from the card and used. They were chosen first, as it was easier to select a matching paper afterwards. The funky paper suits the children and picks out the colours from the photo, bracelet and charm.

The bracelet should sit neatly on the card – try out different measurements between holes on scrap card. When the spacing is correct you can use these holes as a template to mark the position for them on the greeting card.

Birthday wishes

SARAH

I secured the photo directly onto the background paper because the colours blended well. The small plastic flower sequins and flat-backed gems pull the photo and paper together and, as they overlap the photo edges, add a contemporary look. Use non-UPVA glue such as Diamond Glaze to fix these securely.

The fancy metal charm is secured using a small brad so it can be removed, maybe to add to a key ring.

Adapt this card to make a 'Just to say' card for a friend. Imagine the surprise and delight at receiving your spontaneous gesture and the memories that it will bring back.

green for go

Passing your driving test is a big occasion, especially if you have a car ready and waiting to be driven! This card celebrates the achievement and acknowledges the effort put in by the learner.

Card size 14 x 20cm (5½ x 8in)

I cut around the car to eliminate the background, making it stand out from its yellow mat, (chosen to pick out the colour in the brake lights). To make it appear to pop out further I secured it with sticky fixer pads.

To ensure that this card was dynamic with lots of impact and clean lines, I chose geometric paper. I cut the paper to size and then made the card blank a little larger. This avoids cutting through the pattern to fit a standard-size card.

The licence plate was altered using photographic software and adds a humorous play on words. This also doubles up as the card's greeting.

The sentiments on the small tags apply to passing all sorts of exams, so this card can be adapted for other occasions simply by using a relevant photograph.

I cut the small photo and the green mat under the large photo so that they fitted exactly within the pattern of the paper. Use patterns in this way to eliminate the need for accurate measuring!

piece of cake

The image of a cake identifies this as a birthday card in less time than it takes to read the message. The subtle colour scheme of pink and silver gives the card an elegant and feminine look, though you could easily adapt this for a boy.

Card size 11.5 x 18cm (4½ x 7in)

To make the card layout extra special and pick up the silver everywhere else, I added silver ribbon and beads on the far left. Firstly the beads were sewn onto the ribbon with backstitch and then the ribbon was secured to the card using StudioTac tape adhesive. A spot of glue at the base of the last bead ensures the thread will not unravel.

I cropped the sides from the photo to fit the card format and secured it centrally between the left and right edges after the ribbon was attached.

The small shop-bought cup cake is decorated with edible silver balls, a candle and ribbon. I photographed it in front of an A4 sheet of pink card to reflect the colour of the cake and add warmth.

I matted the greeting and photo onto silver card to add definition to the edges.

family christmas

Christmas means bringing family together, however far apart they are, and to make one lucky grandma feel closer here's a very special Christmas card. It's made in the popular square format, which scrapbookers will be familiar with, and you can make two from a standard sheet of scrapbooking card.

A charming picture of brother and sister, taken in front of the family Christmas tree before a party, makes an excellent centrepiece for the front of the card, set off by traditional festive colours. Inside there's a surprise: a specially recorded Christmas message stored in a voice pad. Two happy moments have been caught – one when the photo was taken and another when the message was recorded.

The inside of this unique card holds words both written and spoken. The envelope (see opposite) is made in the same papers. To add a postal address, print onto white paper and stick this to the front. For details on making this type of envelope see page 100.

A special Message just for you!

PRESS

Wishing you a Merry Christmas and a Happy 2006

Variations on the theme

There are many occasions when loved ones would appreciate a personalized card. For a comical birthday card, capture the moment when children are singing 'happy birthday' on the recording device. For New Year wishes stand them in front of a clock showing midnight, pulling party poppers or toasting each other with glasses of lemonade!

You will need

✓ Card maker's tool kit, page 8

✓ 12 x 8.5cm (4¾ x 3½in) coloured photo

✓ 15cm (6in) square red textured card blank

✓ Festive lined paper
  • Two 14cm (5½in) squares
  • 3 x 20cm (1¼ x 8in) strip with vertical stripes
  • 1 x 20cm (½ x 8in) strip, horizontal stripes

✓ Sheet of festive spotted paper

✓ White textured card

✓ 13.5 x 11cm (5¼ x 4¼in) rectangle of red card

✓ Narrow ribbon
  • Three 6cm (2½in) lengths in green
  • Two 6cm (2½in) lengths in red
  • 25cm (10in) length in red
  • 30cm (12in) length in red

✓ Decorative word tiles

✓ Voice pad or message recording device
  with a message recorded on it

✓ Small hole punch and hammer

✓ Use of a computer and printer
  or rubber stamps / rub-on letters

Card size 15cm (6in) square

See also
Techniques,
pages 8–25
Materials,
page 110
Suppliers,
page 111

design decisions

The spotty paper used for the photo mat reminds us of baubles and Christmas lights and helps capture the excitement of the season.

Narrow co-ordinating ribbons tied through punched holes soften the edges of the frame and provide added dimension.

The vertical paper strip is secured off-centre, giving the design a contemporary look. It also leads the eye down the card from the photo to the greeting, linking the two together.

greetings papers

Make your own sentiment papers by purchasing plain spotted or squared paper. Write, stamp or use rub-on letters to add letters to the shapes and spell out your greeting.

To create the card front, cut a rectangle approximately 14 x 10cm (5½ x 4in) from spotted paper, keeping the pattern complete. Trim the photo to fit, leaving one row of spots visible all round. Secure the photo then glue on a word tile. Punch out five holes, fold a short red or green ribbon in half and feed through a hole from the back, creating a loop on top. Thread both ends of the ribbon through the loop and pull tight. Trim the ribbon ends then repeat four more times.

Lay the wider lined paper strip down the card front so that it is 3.5cm (1½in) in from the fold. Lay the photo on top, with an even border on three sides. Use a pencil to mark each corner on the card front. Check that the lined paper strip looks correct and move it if necessary. Use a pencil to mark the card front where both vertical edges of the paper strip cross the top and bottom edges.

Apply double-sided tape down the card front within the marks for the strip. Secure the paper strip and trim away any excess. Use the computer to create a sentiment approximately 9cm (3½in) long and print onto white card. Trim to 2cm (¾in) deep, place word tiles at each end of the text, trim the excess card and glue the tiles in place. Secure centrally on the 1cm (½in) lined paper strip and trim to fit the card.

Lay your wording centrally under the photo then use a pencil to mark its position. Apply double-sided tape across the card front within the pencil marks. Press in place. Secure sticky fixer pads to the back of the frame under the photograph. Line the photo up with the pencil marks made in step 2 and press into place. Erase all pencil marks.

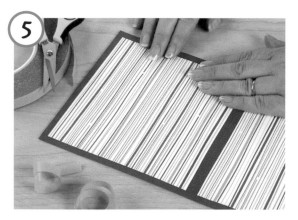

To decorate the inside, first open the card. On the inside left measure 5mm (¼in) from each edge and make a pencil mark. Use double-sided tape to secure one lined paper square, (with the lines vertical), using the pencil marks as guidelines. Repeat for the inside right then erase all the pencil marks carefully.

easy cut

Rather than attempt to cut paper to the exact length of the card I take a longer piece, secure it in place and then trim off the excess with scissors.

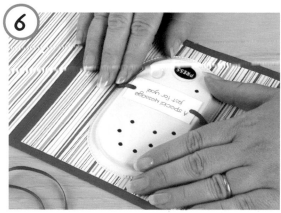

Use the computer to create a tag for the message pad, size it so it fits neatly on the pad, print and trim it. Punch a hole on the left and right sides, thread through the 25cm (10in) length of red ribbon and wrap it round the voice pad. Tie a knot on the left-hand side and trim the ribbon ends at a slant. Secure the voice pad centrally on the inside left using the sticky pads provided.

Use a computer to create a sentiment about 8 x 5cm (3¼ x 2in). Print and trim to approximately 11.5 x 9cm (4½ x 3½in), giving a wide border around the text. Use double-sided tape to secure it to the rectangle of red card and trim. Tie 30cm (12in) of red ribbon around the bottom, tie in a knot at the right-hand side and trim the ends at a slant. Secure centrally on the inside right with double-sided tape.

more to say

Record a longer message on a tape cassette and pop it inside a small envelope secured to the inside of your card. Unlike a phone call these messages can be listened to over and over again.

Full details of the papers and other decorative elements used to make the cards on these pages are provided on page 110.

Square cards offer numerous design options and, as the shape is associated with the popular square scrapbook pages, it is possible to use a down-sized scrapbook layout. Further photos and journaling can be included inside and on the card back.

great skate

The giver of this present was not there when it was opened but the card clearly conveys the delight of the recipient. Photos of the gift and the child using it create a wonderful thank you card. See page 104 for a scrapbook equivalent.

Card size 15cm (6in) square

The scrapbook paper was ideal for the card but too fussy for a small layout so I cut it up and used some of the words plus small sections of the pattern.

Smaller cut-out images of the gift create a fun design and balance the main photo on the left.

The overall look is similar to a crossword with words running both across and down the paper. The words do not interlock but a little careful planning on a piece of paper should enable the design to be taken to this stage.

I chose a photo of the skateboard being used but you could also use a photo of the present being unwrapped.

A contemporary look runs through this design with both the papers and words overlapping.

The shape of the wheel from the skateboard is reflected in the white eyelets securing the words.

This idea is easily adapted for other occasions so try making amusing thank you cards for special wedding or retirement presents. You can also use it to show what you bought with a gift voucher.

life begins at 65

A retirement card is a treasure of all the years spent working alongside a group of friends and colleagues. Heart-felt retirement wishes are enclosed within this very personal and unique card while symbols of what might be achieved in the years ahead are displayed in charms on the card front.

Card size 15cm (6in) square

My aim was to create a neat and organized design with a relatively natural background. I added interest by wrapping faint-lined vellum around the card to produce a loose cover.

Enjoy Your Retirement John
06 09 05

The metal frame and charms were arranged then secured in place using a non-UPVA glue such as Diamond Glaze.

It was easier to stick the sentiment in place prior to cutting and folding the vellum. I laid the vellum over the card with some extra overlap on the right side and estimated where the greeting would start. After sticking on the greeting I laid the vellum back over the card front and adjusted it so the sentiment was central.

Take this idea and create a card for a mum-to-be by securing feeding bottles, dummies and nappy pins around her photo! Instead of charms use buttons and die-cut shapes.

happy memories

As years pass we often find photos of weddings left lying in between the pages of photo albums. Here one such wedding photo has been resurrected to make a very personal and unusual anniversary card.

Card size 15cm (6in) square

Taking inspiration from the bride's veil, I loosely pleated a small piece of white net onto a square of pink card to create a ruched background. Hi-Tack double-sided tape along each edge kept the net temporarily in place as I did this. Alternatively, you could add a piece of material from one of the garments in your photo.

Each edge of net is covered by a strip of lace hand sewn through all layers and secured with seed beads. The pattern of the lace determined where to sew each bead. To avoid mitring the corners I covered each with an artificial flower.

The photo is mounted on white card with pink ribbon wrapped around two corners and is secured at each corner with a seed bead sewn through all the layers.

To see the insert inside this card, turn to page 24.

Still keeping with the wedding-veil theme, half a dozen small silver hearts, (silver peel-offs secured back to back), are caught in the net, resembling wedding confetti. You could also use charms, punched shapes or real confetti.

creative christening

A christening or baptism is usually the first big occasion in a child's life. Along with birth congratulations, christening cards are kept and cherished. Later in life the child can look at the beautiful cards sent to them on their special day.

Card size 15cm (6in) square

To give the impression of a soft quilt under the baby I created a simple patchwork design by sticking pastel-coloured self-adhesive vellum squares onto white card.

It was important that the photo was clearly distinguished from the pattern underneath so to create a definite break between the two I kept a narrow white border around it when I trimmed it to size. You can create a similar effect by mounting your photo on white card.

A little more decoration adds depth and texture without overpowering the photo. I glued toning pastel buttons to the patchwork and under the photo spelt the child's name in clear beads threaded onto wire.

Softness is added with fluffy pink fibre wrapped around the edges and kept in place by notches created using a craft punch.

To see the insert inside this card, turn to page 23.

The decorated white card is linked to the card blank by using pastel-coloured vellum strips secured along each edge. I chose to overlap the strips at the corners but you could mitre them.

ghouls' night out

Ghosts, ghouls, witches, black cats and pumpkins signify that Halloween is upon us, so whip up some spooky invitations featuring these terrifying motifs to get everyone in the mood for your party. To set the scene, this card has a panoramic format that provides space for lots of different images. Normally such a card would have a top fold but I find that long cards like this tend to open up and eventually do the splits. To get around the problem I have designed a card with folds at the bottom, giving it a stable base.

This design has clean, simple lines which means it can be completed speedily, and to save even more time I printed the party details from my computer. If you have a lot of invites to produce you could set up a mini production line involving the whole family. And remember that each invite can be different – there is no rule that says they must all be exactly the same.

Variations on the theme

Adapt this card for Thanksgiving by using photos of autumn, a cornucopia, fruit or corn. Turn it over and write your own Thanksgiving grace or recipe on the back. Alternatively, use photos of family members and send special wishes to a friend or relative who can't share the celebration with you. You could even use photos from your party to create a 'We Missed You' card to send after the event.

Made from pieces of black and orange card, this envelope matches the invitation inside. As it has been made for hand delivery there isn't any name on it, just a warning! For full details on making this type of envelope, see page 100.

you will need

✓ Card maker's tool kit, page 8
✓ Four 5 x 7.5cm (2 x 3in) coloured photos
✓ Black card
  • 27 x 30cm (10½ x 12in) rectangle
  • Leftover pieces
✓ Orange card
  • 27 x 2.5cm (10½ x 1in) strip
  • 27 x 6.5cm (10½ 2½in) strip
  • 27 x 13.5cm (10½ x 5¼in) rectangle
✓ Cassette craft punch (letters)
✓ Halloween buttons
✓ Use of a computer and printer

Card size 27 x 13.5cm (10½ x 5¼in)

See also
Techniques,
pages 8–25
Materials,
page 110
Suppliers,
page 111

design decisions

The punched stencil letters
recall the pumpkin carving
associated with Halloween.

*You could use one photo on
the front, but when there
are several to choose from
simply reduce their size to
fit and use three or four.*

*Ready-made
embellishments such
as fancy buttons add
appropriate decoration and
dimension quickly.*

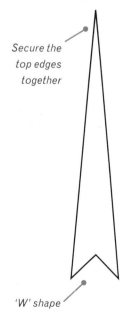

*Secure the
top edges
together*

'W' shape

*Create the above shape
for your card by following
steps 1 and 2.*

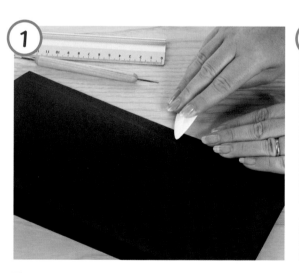

To create the card blank, measure from the left 13.5cm (5¼in) across the longest edge of the large black card then score with a stylus and ruler. Still from the left measure 15cm (6in) across and score again. Finally make a third measurement of 16.5cm (6¾in) and score. With the wrong sides of the card together fold along the central scored line.

Crease each outer scored line well with a bone folder, folding the card so that the central fold is facing upwards and the two outer folds are facing downwards. This creates an 'W' shape that will become a stand for the card. Ensure the right side of the card is on the outside then secure the top (unfolded) edges of the card together using double-sided tape.

For the front decoration punch out 'Happy Halloween' with the cassette craft punch from leftover black card. Use scissors to cut around each letter to give straight edges of varying angles.

Lay out the letters on the 2.5cm (1in) strip of orange card and arrange neatly. Glue each letter in place then glue a witch button into the space between the words.

word spacing

It can be difficult to space cut-out letters and words evenly. One trick is to secure the letters of the first word then start with the last letter of the second word and work backwards. Make a feature of the gap between the words by securing a button or other embellishment within it.

Secure the four photos at varying angles on the 6.5cm (2½in) orange strip of card using sticky fixer pads. The photos should overlap each other and the card edges.

Use double-sided tape to secure the greeting strip on the card front 5mm (¼in) down from the top edge. Secure the photo strip in the same way 1cm (½in) up from the bottom edge. Add further decoration by gluing on more buttons.

scary font

There are an infinite number of computer fonts available so instead of punching out the letters why not have a look to see if there is an appropriate font you can use.

Use the space on the back of the card to add details of the party, embellishing it with leftover buttons and appropriate stickers, as desired.

For the card back type the party invitation on your computer and print onto the 13.5cm (5¼in) wide orange card. Add a punched title and other decorations, trim the card to size and secure to the back of the card with double-sided tape.

GHOULS NIGHT OUT

Halloween hubble bubble, toil and trouble begins at 7pm. Put your scariest costume on then hitch a ride on a broomstick, or catch the Graveyard Express to 16 Courtyard Close.

Witches Brew, Goblin Crisps, Pumpkin Pie and lots of other Monster Snacks will be provided. Please feel free to bring along a bottle, or two, of your own poison!

We hope you can make it. Creepily Yours, The "Goosebumps" Family (012 345 6789)

more occasions

A panoramic format enables you to experiment with unusual design layouts and include landscape-format photos. You could even try cutting an aperture in the front prior to construction and then dangle a photo within it.

easter bunny

Lemon and green are the colours of spring and are used here to create a stunning card sending Easter wishes. The photo of the little rabbit nestling between the daffodils adds a cute touch. See also the scrapbook version on page 105.
Card size 30 x 13cm (12 x 5in)

Lemon is the dominant colour in this design so to pick up the leaf green and add definition to the edges of the paper I wrapped green sheer ribbon around the top and bottom. Toning alphabet stickers overlay the ribbon.

I used paper with daffodils in the top half and hydrangeas at the bottom, which I trimmed so that I could use the daffodils on the front and the hydrangeas on the back.

The images leant themselves beautifully to decoupage. By using extra sheets I created a three-dimensional effect on two of the daffodil blooms and the butterfly. Leftover paper can be used to create smaller Easter cards.

I secured the paper to the back with double-sided tape on three sides to form a side-opening pocket. The greeting is written on a tag, decorated with stickers and popped into the pocket.

merci

It is wonderful to receive a bouquet and the thought behind the gift is reflected in the beauty of the flowers, but when you order flowers for a friend far away you don't get to see the bouquet you paid for. This thank you card enables the giver to take equal pleasure in the gift, because it features a photo of the pretty bouquet.
Card size 20 x 13cm (8 x 5in)

The close-up photo of the blooms was cut using the Coluzzle cutting system. A larger yellow mat picks up the colour of the sunflowers.

The mesh adds a textured finish to the card background and is also reminiscent of the gypsophila found in many flower arrangements. Cellophane bouquet wrapping is often pretty so you could also use this.

A small wooden sunflower, placed in the top corner, was all that was needed to balance the design but you could also incorporate a few dried flowers from the bouquet (a microwave flower press can dry the flowers in seconds).

I used white ribbon from the bouquet to help break up the expanse of lilac background and lift the white from the mesh. Placed just along two sides it also adds a nice contemporary feel.

The thank you letter is written on thin card and folded into three then its central panel is secured to the card back with double-sided tape. A beaded closure keeps the letter shut.

dashing dad

Why not make a special Father's Day card that can be kept on display all year round? This is a wonderful way to capture a moment in time to bring back memories of the fun you had together.

Card size 24 x 14.5cm (9½ x 5¾in)

Green paper and card bring out the different shades of green in the photo's background. The burgundy paper, which warms and lifts the green, comes from the same paper range for the perfect complement.

Metal embellishments add depth and stability as well as a masculine touch.

Secured to the card back is an envelope created from the same paper as the main design. A letter or more photographs can be popped into this.

Woven tags effortlessly add an interesting texture to the layout. I used the tag along with the metal plaque to express feelings without being overly sentimental.

Overlaying papers add interest without complication. Entwining and overlaying papers can also be used to demonstrate family or emotional ties between two subjects in the photo.

A strip of paper just secured to the top of the envelope is passed through two slits in the bottom half to keep it closed.

gone but not forgotten

It is an emotional time when a long-term friend moves away. Those left behind can console each other but the one who leaves often has to start again by making new friends. This card will remind them of the times spent with you.

Card size 29 x 13cm (11¼in x 5in)

This group photo was taken especially for the card and is very natural. The location is important because this is where the friends meet up.

The colours of card and paper were determined by the name of the shop, Crimson Crafts. I used striped paper for interest and because I could alter the direction of the stripes from horizontal to vertical.

The vellum 'Friends' was originally white so colour was added to the back with marker pens.

The vellum strip was printed on the computer and secured across the photo.

To personalize the card I asked each person to write a sentiment around the photo. To ensure longevity they used an acid-free pen.

The back of the card provides information about the time and place of the photo plus some humorous snippets to make the recipient smile.

21st birthday

Greetings cards for men can be quite a challenge but for a special occasion such as a 21st birthday it's worth spending a little extra time to create something distinctive. This card has an unusual construction that creates endless possibilities for decorating with photographs, papers and embellishments. It is divided into three sections across the width and you can embellish the whole thing. The left panel folds over to the right in a concertina fold so that when closed you can see the left panel and half of the right-hand panel as one. The whole card stands firmly when opened to reveal all the decorations and sentiments.

As his favourite hobby, football had to be the theme for this recipient, and the card features a photo of him showing off his skills. I wanted to include more photos but this was the only one of him in football strip so I incorporated readily available photo stickers instead.

An enveloped made from football paper is the ideal finishing touch and was made from leftover paper and stickers. For full details on making this type of envelope see page 100.

Variations on the theme

This card is easily adapted to suit all sorts of other sports or hobbies including swimming, gardening, baking, surfing or fishing. Just choose whatever the recipient likes best. You could even make a card for a crafter that incorporates photos of her finished projects, works in progress or workroom.

you will need

✓ Card maker's tool kit, page 8
✓ 6 x 12cm (2¼ x 4¾in) coloured photo
✓ 28 x 14cm (11 x 5½in) black card rectangle
✓ Off-cut of blue card
✓ Soccer ball design paper
  • 14 x 12cm (5½ x 4¾in) rectangle
  • 6 x 12cm (2¼ x 4¾in) rectangle
✓ Photo stickers or extra photos
✓ Dynamo Junior embossed label maker with
  black tape

**Card size 28 x 14cm (11 x 5½in) folded down
to 14cm (5½in) square**

See also
Techniques,
pages 8–25
Materials,
page 110
Suppliers,
page 111

design decisions

Dynamo labelling tape complements the youthful design with embossed greetings and text.

Although decorative paper provides a background for the photo stickers the main photo is secured directly onto the card blank. This provides a plain frame around it to make this image more prominent than the others.

Matting the photo stickers onto blue card links them to the main photo by picking up the colour of the footballer's socks.

---

front view

Always keep in mind how your design will look when the card is closed and the left half of the large panel is covered by the far left panel.

To make the side-fold card, measure 14cm (5½in) across from the right-hand side of the black card rectangle and score with a stylus. Again from the right-hand side, measure across 21cm (8¼in) and score with a stylus. Crease well along both scored lines using a bone folder.

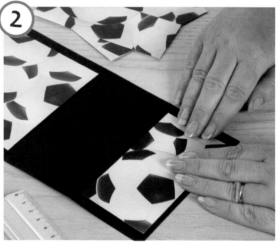

For the decoration first secure the background papers using double-sided tape. Stick the larger rectangle of soccer ball paper to the right-hand panel 1cm (⅜in) from both the top and bottom edges. Stick the second rectangle of soccer ball paper to the left-hand panel so it is 5mm (¼in) in from each side and lined up with the top and bottom edges of the first paper.

3

Mat three square photo stickers onto blue card (mine were 4.5cm (1¾in) square). Choose a rectangular sticker and check it will fit nicely on the card then mat it onto blue card. My sticker was 7 x 8.5cm (2¾ x 3¼in), which I trimmed down to 5.5cm (2⅛in) wide. Use the guillotine method to trim the mats to a narrow border (see page 13).

4

Create the text using the label maker. Create one sticker with the date of the main photo. Make the 'Happy' label with extra tape after the text and the 'Birthday' and '21 today' labels with extra tape before the text.

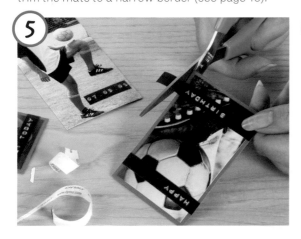

5

Stick the date tape onto the main photo and the '21 today' tape across the ball photo sticker. Trim any excess tape. Position the 'happy' and 'birthday' tapes in the same way.

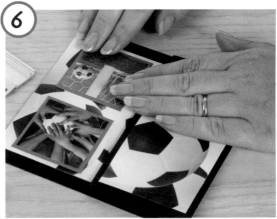

6

Add the photo and stickers, starting with the largest area on the right-hand side and spacing them evenly. Mark the card with your measurements in pencil to help with placement.

7

Position the third sticker so that it balances the other two. This must not extend more than 7cm (2¾in) from the fold otherwise it will be seen when the card is closed. Erase all pencil marks.

8

Secure the main photo centrally, 5mm (¼in) from each fold, on the undecorated panel, lining up the top and bottom edges with the papers. Secure the remaining photo centrally on the remaining panel.

neat fold

When securing paper up to a valley fold ensure that it is a fraction to the side of it. The card will then shut easily as the glue and paper will not restrict it.

through a window

A nice idea is to cut an aperture through both left panels so that part of the design on the right panel can be seen when the card is closed.

more occasions

Adding a side fold to a conventional card results in it becoming more dimensional. You can alter it by moving the centre front fold further to the left or right or by adding in a second fold to the left panel.

Full details of the papers and other decorative elements used to make the cards on these pages are provided on page 110.

wedded bliss

This idea makes a smashing wedding anniversary card. Use a photo taken at the wedding and enhance the layout with pretty co-ordinating papers, stick-on sentiments and sheer ribbon. The result is a beautiful keepsake card.

Card size 29 x 20cm (11½ x 8in) folded down to 17 x 20cm (7 x 8in)

When closed, the pretty design on the paper is continued from the left panel across the fold to the right. I achieved this seamless effect by ensuring that the pattern on the left panel was exactly the same as the pattern hidden from view when the card is closed.

Rekindle long forgotten memories and share your anniversary date by sending a 'Do You Remember' card to your bridesmaid, best man or usher. Imagine their surprise when they open the envelope to find a photo of themselves taken at your wedding staring back at them.

I wanted to include a poem and sourced this one written by George Elliot. I printed it onto the co-ordinating striped paper using a font similar to that in the stickers. Using brown ink instead of black gives a much softer overall effect.

I threaded and tied sheer cream ribbon through eyelets to add a delicate touch in keeping with the style of paper. Each end of the ribbon ties is cut at a slant.

The pretty word stickers have a touch of glitter, adding a little sparkle to the overall design. Although these came from a wedding celebration pack they are also ideal sentiments for an anniversary.

The photo was cut into an oval using the Coluzzle cutting system and then mounted on a larger oval cut from co-ordinating striped paper. It sits nicely on the far right of the card, looking well balanced both when the card is closed and open.

remember when

Why wait for a special occasion to send a card? This fun and funky card is a fantastic way to say hello while bringing back memories of a fun time. Although these papers are very bright they complement the photo and do not overpower it.

Card size 28 x 20cm (11 x 8in) folded down to 14cm (5½ x 8in)

When it is closed, the card shows a picture of the person who sent the card with the jolly 'hello' greeting on a tag.

Although brown card was not my original choice for the background I found that the dark colour worked well with the bright busy paper. Always hold your paper against a few different choices of background before making your final decision.

The co-ordinating tags were a quick way to add more decoration while retaining the retro appeal of the card.

The photo background is secured using sticky fixer pads along three sides to create a pocket for a tag. The tag has another message, adding to the fun element of this card.

Instead of people, use photos of places that are easily divided into two halves. Or take your own specially arranged photos where you have deliberately separated items by placing them onto two different colours of card.

White and pale blue fibres threaded with random white pearlized beads add texture and movement to the card. The needle big enough for the thread was too thick for the beads so I got around this by threading each bead onto it using a needle threader.

As the background in the photo didn't work with the colours in the papers, I trimmed around the images to remove it. However the images then became lost when held directly against the paper so I created another background, picking up the green of the paper.

you're one today!

We love baby photographs and this super pocket card enables you to display four of the best. Its clever construction means that you can easily take out the individual photo cards for a closer look.

This pocket card commemorates all those special firsts that happen within a child's first twelve months and it makes a very special birthday card that can go on to be enjoyed and treasured forever. Each pretty pocket contains a small card and photo that records the time and place of the event in the picture.

This card was presented to Grace on her first birthday with the last mini card left blank. Her parents completed the card by adding a photo taken on the big day. The card is presented in a co-ordinating box that provides storage for years to come (see page 102 for instructions on making the presentation box).

variations on the theme

You don't have to choose exactly the same subjects for your card as I did. You could use any series of images that show different stages in a baby's first year or periods in the life of an older child or adult. Try a selection of school photos for a graduation card or fun photos for a teenage birthday. Instead of mini cards you can pop postcards or envelopes in the pockets (see the variations on pages 54–55).

Bathin

Precious Little One

you will need

✓ Card maker's tool kit, page 8

✓ Four 8 x 10cm (3¼ x 4in) photos

✓ Co-ordinating paper rectangles:
  - (A) green with pink spot – two 10.5 x 20cm (4¼ x 8in)
  - (B) green with pink pattern – two 10.5 x 20cm (4¼ x 8in)
  - (C) stripe – four 13 x 5.5cm (5⅛ x 2⅛in)
  - (D) pale pink – two 9 x 17cm (3½ x 6¾in)
  - (E) pale pink chequered – two 9 x 17cm (3½ x 6¾in)
  - (F) dark pink paper

✓ Four 8.5 x 16cm (3¼ x 6¼in) white card blanks

✓ Sizzix Die Cutting System with System Converter or Sizzix SideKick

✓ Sizzix Sizzlets Alphabet – Script

✓ Xyron with permanent adhesive cartridge

✓ Large oval craft punch 7.5cm (3in) high

✓ Green chequered card rectangles
  - (G) 24.5 x 20cm (9¾ x 8in)
  - (H) 23 x 20cm (9 x 8in)

✓ Green spotted card rectangles
  - (I) four 6.5 x 10.5cm (2½ x 4⅛in)

**Card size 46 x 20cm (18 x 8in)
folded down to 11.5 x 20cm (4½ x 8in)**

design decisions

The hearts above the apertures link the cards and draw attention to the photographs.

The papers chosen for the mini cards complement each other and enhance the photographs.

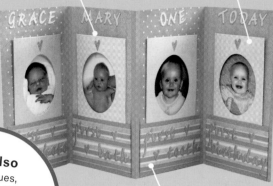

See also
Techniques,
pages 8–25
Materials,
page 110
Suppliers,
page 111

Use the main colour for the letters and the secondary colour for the shadows. The shadows lift the letters away from the background, making them more visible, while the hearts fill the different line lengths and provide a link to the mini cards.

paper packs

Co-ordinated paper packs take the guesswork out of mixing and matching colours and patterns. They also encourage your creativity by providing you with colours and patterns that you might not select if purchasing sheets individually.

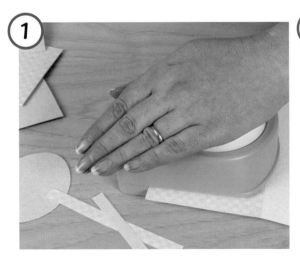

To make the mini cards, apply Xyron adhesive to the plain and squared pale pink rectangles, D and E. Cut each to the same size as the front of the mini card blanks, remove the backing paper and press in place. Add an aperture to each mini card by making a faint pencil mark 1cm (⅜in) down from the centre of the top edge. Line up the outside of the oval craft punch with this mark and punch out. Erase the pencil marks using the soft putty rubber.

Apply Xyron adhesive to the dark pink paper, F. Punch out eleven hearts and use a pricking tool or pin to remove the backing paper. Secure one heart above each aperture. Put the remaining hearts to one side for the moment.

3

Position a photo inside each card behind the aperture and trim to fit. Apply double-sided tape to the back of each one and secure in place.

4

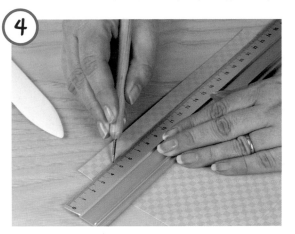

To make the main card, create two panels on each of the green chequered backing cards, G and H. From the left-hand side on both rectangles, measure across 11.5cm (4½in), score and fold. Create a flap on the larger rectangle by measuring, scoring and folding 1cm (⅜in) in from the right-hand (wider) side.

5

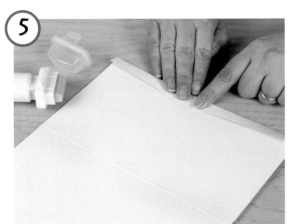

With the right side facing upwards apply glue to the flap, right up to the scored line. Lay the other rectangle on top with its right side facing downwards. Line up the top, bottom and right-hand edges, and ensure that the left-hand side is butted against the scored line. Secure the flap by pressing it down onto the card. Hold the flap in place for a minute while the glue dries.

6

Decorate the main card by adding the four green papers A and B to the middle of each panel. Take one of the striped papers (C) and wrap it around the middle of one of the green spotted card rectangles (I) creasing well. Remove then secure in place with double-sided tape. Apply double-sided tape to the sides and bottom then secure on the card rectangle to make a pocket. Repeat three more times.

7

Apply Xyron adhesive to leftover dark green card and pink paper. Use the Sizzix alphabet set to die cut the letters and shadows. Remove the backing paper from each letter and apply it to the correct shadow. Lay the letters on your card and arrange. Remove the backing paper from each shadow and apply to the pockets and card using tweezers. In the gaps secure the hearts put to one side in step 2.

tape deductions

When creating cards to your own measurements, ensure that you take into account that the width of the double-sided tape reduces the inside width of the pocket.

quick cut

Prior to die cutting your letters, write out the text on scrap paper and add up how many of each letter you need. It saves time if you cut all that you need of each letter in turn.

This attractive presentation box was created using more of the card materials and one of the ovals removed in step 1. See page 102 for full instructions.

more occasions

You can use the joining pages on this card to show four events, but if this doesn't suit your needs you could extend the card to six or even eight pages. The pockets are perfect for any detachable photographs or keepsakes.

Full details of the papers and embellishments used for the cards on these pages are provided on page 110.

a great grandpa

Bring together photos of each grandchild and create a wonderful card that any grandparent would be overjoyed to receive. Before sending, ask the children to write a message on the bottom of their postcard using a metallic gel pen.

Card size 46 x 20cm (18 x 8in)
folded down to 11.5 x 20cm (4½ x 8in)

As each photo was very different in colour and background, I converted them all to black and white for continuity. I eliminated the unwanted background by cropping each one down to focus on the child's face.

This card could easily be adapted to send warm wishes to a family member or friend who is working overseas.

As the card is from children I added in a fun element by using funky metal alphabet bottle caps to spell their names. The metal theme is further complemented by the heart brad fixed through each photo.

This card is for a man so I used a pack of complementary striped papers and avoided very fussy designs. The colours gave a cheerful look to the card and therefore enabled me to further enhance the photos by introducing black.

The torn paper gives a rugged and contemporary look to the overall design.

happy mother's day

Pep up the gift of some vouchers by creating a personal Mother's Day card and decorating envelopes for the vouchers to go inside. It's ideal if you can't visit on this special day. Adapt the card to suit the type of vouchers you are sending.

Card size 48 x 18.5cm (19 x 7½in)
folded down to 12 x 18.5cm (4¾ x 7½in)

By matting the photo twice I was able to bring in two more colours: the green from the backing card and the lilac from the papers.

For a soft look, fluffy eyelash fibre is tied around the greeting card and through the die cut tags on the envelopes.

I selected the most dominant colour from the paper for the small tags.

This mother was likely to spend her vouchers on fashion accessories, so that determined the type of images to use on the card.

I sought out the two complementary patterned papers and let these determine the remaining colours for my card. One paper was used to create the pockets and the other to mat onto the shop-bought envelopes.

Shiny silver dots placed at the corners of each pocket and sprinkled randomly on them add a little glitz. The photos on the tags are also enhanced with shiny silver dots that are placed on the handbag buckle, flower centres and shoe bows.

I used a craft punch to round the corners once the backing card was assembled.

more occasions 55

thank you

Like French windows, the doors on a front-opening card open outwards, revealing photographs, journaling and embellishments. It's ideal for those occasions when you want to give someone special an extra-big thank you because it provides such a large area for decoration. It is also easily adaptable for many other celebrations and festivities (see pages 60–61).

In this case Charlotte wanted to thank her friend Val for making her beautiful wedding dress. The simple lines of the layout echo the elegance of the dress and the lovely floral papers mirror its colours and add a romantic touch.

The envelope is created using another design from the pretty paper collection used on the card. Suitable for hand delivery only, this envelope wraps around the card and is held together with a length of ribbon (which matches the ribbon used on the card) threaded through holes in the top and bottom flaps. For full details on making this type of envelope see page 98.

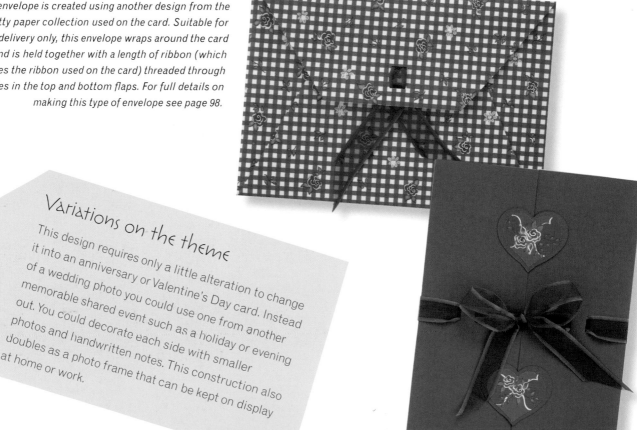

Variations on the theme

This design requires only a little alteration to change it into an anniversary or Valentine's Day card. Instead of a wedding photo you could use one from another memorable shared event such as a holiday or evening out. You could decorate each side with smaller photos and handwritten notes. This construction also doubles as a photo frame that can be kept on display at home or work.

To My Dear Friend Val,
A very big thank you for
making me such a
wonderful wedding
dress. It was so much
more than I ever
imagined and I felt
fabulous wearing it.

Charlotte & Steve
28th August 2004

Steve and I had a
fantastic day and we are
so glad that you were
able to join us.
With much love and
thanks,
Charlotte X
17th September 2004

you will need

✓ Card maker's tool kit, page 8
✓ 7.5 x 12.5cm (3 x 5in) colour photo
✓ Moss green textured card
  • 30 x 20cm (12 x 8in) rectangle
  • Two 6.5 x 19.5cm (2½ x 7¾in) rectangles
✓ Pink, green and white floral paper
  • 13.5 x 19.5cm (5¼ x 7¾in) rectangle with the pattern running horizontally
  • 11.5 x 17.5cm (4½ x 7in) rectangle with the pattern running vertically
✓ White paper cut with a deckle edge
  • 12 x 18cm (4¾ x 7¼in) rectangle
  • 8 x 13cm (3¼ x 5¼in) rectangle
✓ Leftovers from your chosen papers
✓ 70cm (28in) of 1.5cm (⅝in) wide pink ribbon
✓ Two 25cm (10in) lengths of thin white ribbon
✓ Engraved brass 'thank you'
✓ Sizzix personal die-cutting machine with hearts (38-0157) and bookplates (38-1055)
✓ Sizzix lacing (38-0849) punch
✓ Two white eyelets
✓ Use of a computer and printer

Card size 28 x 20cm (11 x 8in)
folded down to 14 x 20cm
(5½ x 8in)

See also
Techniques, pages 8–25
Materials, page 110
Suppliers, page 111

design decisions

The white mats behind the photo and decorative paper appear to lift them off their backgrounds and brighten the pink and green colours.

Die-cut hearts add instant decoration.

Using one sheet of paper for the double mat and alternating the direction of the pattern gives the appearance of using co-ordinating papers.

The thin white ribbon behind the hearts echoes the wavy white lines on the floral paper and provides a change of texture.

perfect alignment

To line up the ribbon holes punched in step 2, punch the first holes then mark the handle of the punch where it crosses the bottom edge of the card. Use this to position the punch precisely on the other side.

ribbon option

If you don't want to invest in the Sizzix paddle punch you can omit the lacing holes. Fold the ribbon in half and glue it to the centre of the card back. Conceal the glue by covering it with a die-cut heart.

To make the front-opening card blank
measure 7cm (2¾in) in from the left-hand side of the large green card, score using a stylus and crease well with a bone folder. This creates the front-left panel. Measure 21cm (8¼in) from the left-hand side, score using a stylus and crease well with a bone folder. Fold the front right over the card back and mark with a pencil where the left front folds over onto it. Trim the excess away from the right-hand side.

Open out the card and measure 3.5cm (1½in) in from the left-hand side along the bottom edge; mark with a pencil. Measure and mark 10cm (4in) up from this. Lay the card on a cutting mat with the paddle punch on top and adjust so that you can see the second pencil mark through the hole nearest the card edge. Hit with a hammer to punch out the ribbon holes then repeat for the right-hand side. Cut one end of the ribbon on a slant and thread the ribbon through the holes.

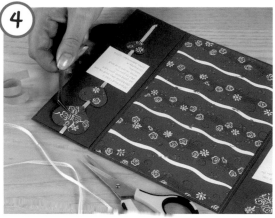

For the card front die-cut two large green hearts and two medium floral hearts. Glue a paper heart to each card heart. Make a pencil mark 3cm (1½in) down the right edge of the card front and stick half the heart on the card with the top mid-point at the mark. Attach the other heart symmetrically. Secure a brass 'thank you' to the bottom-right.

To decorate the inside use double-sided tape to secure the large floral paper to the inside back. Die-cut two small, two medium and two large hearts from leftover floral paper. Type two separate pieces of text about 5cm (2in) wide. Print onto leftover white paper and trim, leaving a narrow border. Glue the top of one 25cm (10in) long white ribbon to the back of a small green rectangle, lay it down the front then glue the hearts and text over it. Use double-side tape to secure the card to the left inside panel. Repeat for the right-hand side.

Use double-sided tape to mat the 11.5cm (4½in) patterned paper onto the large rectangle of deckle edged white paper. Mat the photo onto the small rectangle of deckle-edged white paper.

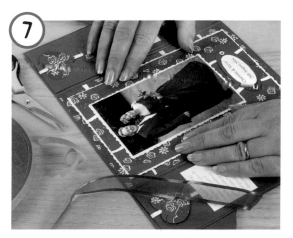

Die-cut a bookplate from leftover green card. Type the names of the bride, groom and wedding date on a computer. Print a draft copy, check the text fits within the label and adjust if required. Print again onto the white paper in a toning colour and use the die-cutting template method to cut the bookplate text (see page 19). Glue the label and text below the photo and then set off each hole with a white eyelet.

Using double-sided tape, secure the double mat you have been working on centrally onto the card. Close the card and tie the ribbon ends in a pretty bow to finish.

measuring template

When making cards in bulk a template saves valuable time. To help mark the position of the ribbon holes, cut a piece of scrap card to 3.5 x 10cm (1¼ x 4in) and place this on the card front. Line it up with the bottom edge and the card fold then mark with a pencil where the top corner touches the card.

fancy edges

Giving paper a decorative edge adds interest and there are a wide variety of decorative cutting blades and scissors available. I chose to use a deckle edge as it is a random pattern that requires no matching at the corners.

A front-opening card provides a large area that can be decorated but hidden from view until the card is opened out. Decorate the closed card in a way that will draw the recipient in.

Full details of the papers and other decorative elements used to make the cards on these pages are provided on page 110.

santa's little helper

Make an amusing Christmas card using a photo of your pet wearing a Santa hat! If he won't wear a hat then give him some tinsel or pop him in a present sack. Take a little time to have some fun with your pet and your photos will reflect this.

Card size 28 x 17cm (11 x 6¾in) folding down to 14 x 17cm (5½ x 6¾in)

I wanted to give the recipient a sneak preview so I punched a square aperture in one side front. When the card is closed the dog's face can be seen through the window.

The journaling and greeting are written on the back of the card.

A garland of page bubbles and red stars fills an empty space in the photo and ties in with the garland on the far left. The red stone on the dog's collar ensures the main image is glitzy too.

The pattern on the decorative paper has wavy edges. Instead of a straight edge at the sides I decided to cut along the pattern lines.

The aperture idea can be used to highlight any area of a card. Try the candle on a cake, a baby's foot or a toddler's toothy grin.

Patterned ribbon ties pick up the colours of the card and add a decorative element. As the aperture is central the ribbon is tied at top and bottom.

I wanted to have a wide border on one side for the decorations and decided to place the photo over to the right so that the dog is looking towards the centre. This gave me a nice wide border to decorate on the left.

Die-cut dog bones decorated with self-adhesive red stones add a quirky element and double as photo corners.

Make the image of the dog pop out from the background by using two copies of the photo. Trim one into a rectangle, mat it onto red card and secure over the larger photo. You can also use this technique to create one image from two different photos or to eliminate items from a background.

birthday keepsake

Young children love to see photos of themselves so this card, which features photos taken throughout the previous year, is bound to delight the recipient, birthday-boy Joshua. It can be treasured as a keepsake for years to come.

Card size 44 x 27cm (17⅜ x 10½in) folded down to 22 x 27cm (8¾ x 10½in)

A photo of Joshua is matted onto a separate piece of card that is only secured to the front right-hand side. This gives an alternative to the effect created by both sides meeting in the middle.

The named zipper pull is a fun addition that can be removed and hooked onto a coat zip afterwards.

This idea of capturing a year in time works well for celebrating birthdays of most ages. You can also lengthen the time period for a milestone anniversary card so it picks out photos from important lifetime events.

The letters, text and pictures came from a mix-and-match paper/embellishment pack, taking the guesswork out of co-ordination. The title, Joshua, has been given extra definition by matting each letter onto the same card used for the side panels.

The photos on either side of the centre are secured onto cards that have been used to create pockets. In each pocket is a tag with journaling about the event (see page 21).

I decorated the back of the front flap although you could also use this area to write your greeting.

The oversize card was created from three panels. I made a feature of this by using different coloured card for the side panels. I cut the two side panels a little wider to create a flap for double-sided tape then secured each one to the centre panel.

I achieved a fun element by having text that overlaps photos as well as small tags secured with colourful eyelets.

Staples are a novel way of securing card and paper. The metallic ones used here come in a variety of colours although you could colour standard staples prior to use with a permanent marker.

it's a boy!

As if enclosing something very precious, the panels of this card close carefully over the card front with ribbon ties, while revealing a tantalizing glimpse of the contents. This is a novel variation of the front-opening card shown on page 56 that is just so appropriate for a new birth card.

This special card has been lovingly created for someone special. It could be by the mother for the proud grandparents or made as a keepsake by the grandmother for the new mum. The top edges of the card front are cut at an angle to provide a diamond shape where the baby's photo is placed. The remainder of the card stays hidden and tied closed with sheer ribbon. Inside the card are details of the baby's name, birth date, weight and length.

Cut from two pieces of paper, this envelope is large enough to accommodate the full size card made from a single sheet of 12 x 12in paper. The closure at the bottom of the envelope has been made into a feature by using leftover decorations. It is suitable for hand delivery only because the top is unsealed. For full details on making this type of envelope see page 100.

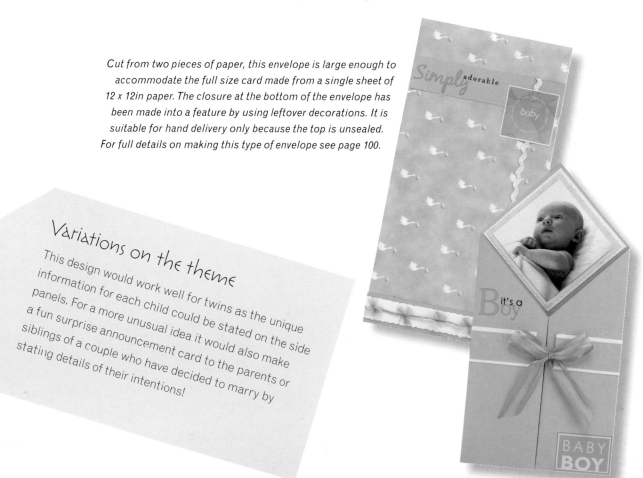

Variations on the theme

This design would work well for twins as the unique information for each child could be stated on the side panels. For a more unusual idea it would also make a fun surprise announcement card to the parents or siblings of a couple who have decided to marry by stating details of their intentions!

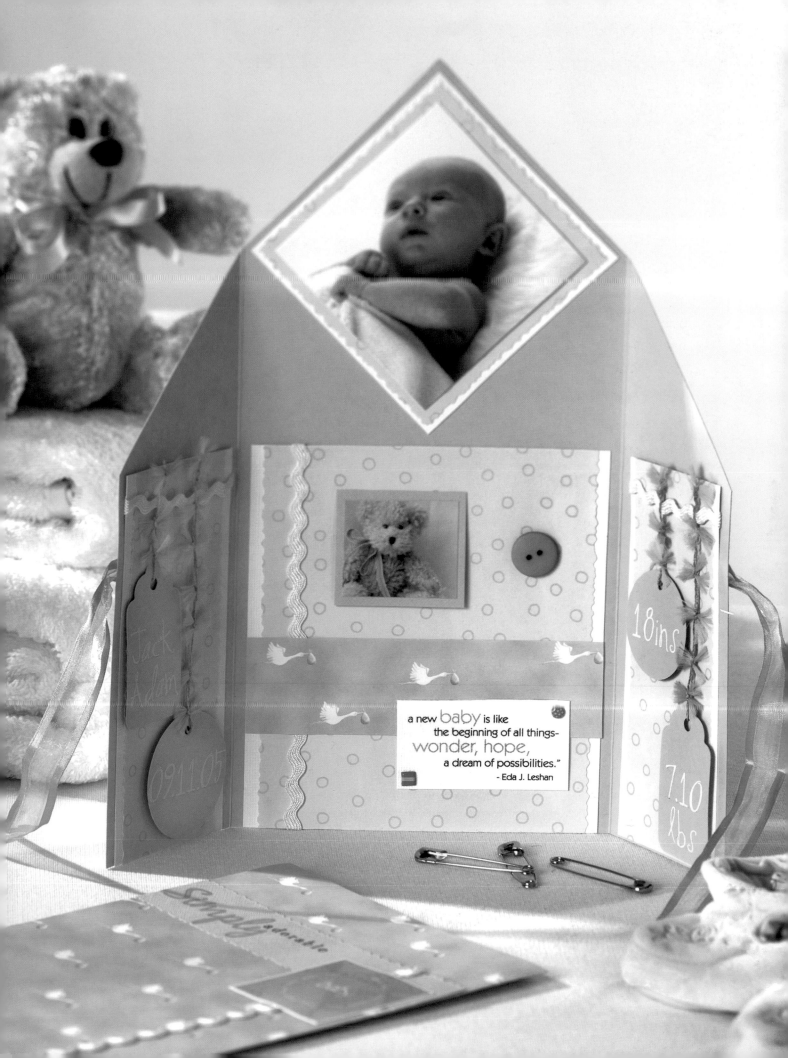

a new baby is like
the beginning of all things-
wonder, hope,
a dream of possibilities."
- Eda J. Leshan

Jack
Adam

09.11.05

18ins

7.10
lbs

Simply adorable

you will need

- ✓ Card maker's tool kit, page 8
- ✓ 8.5cm (3⅜in) square black and white photo
- ✓ Pale blue textured card
  - 30cm (12in) square
  - 15cm (6in) square
- ✓ White textured card
  - Two 3.5 x 6.5cm (1⅜ x 2½in) rectangles
  - Two 6.5 x 15cm (2½ x 6in) strips
  - 14 x 15cm (5½ x 6in) rectangle
  - 10cm (4in) square
- ✓ Circle-patterned blue paper
  - Two 5.5 x 15cm (2¼ x 6in) strips
  - 13 x 15cm (5 x 6in) rectangle
  - 9.5cm (3¾in) square
- ✓ 4 x 14cm (1½ x 5½in) stork patterned paper
- ✓ Four 25cm (10in) lengths of wired blue fibre
- ✓ White rickrack braid cut into two 10cm (4in) lengths and one 20cm (8in) length
- ✓ 45cm (18in) length of sheer pale blue ribbon
- ✓ Photo sticker and baby/alphabet rub-ons
- ✓ Blue button and two decorative brads
- ✓ Small hole punch
- ✓ Sizzix tag and circle dies and embossing folder (border, dots 38-9512)

Card size 15 x 30cm (6 x 12in)

See also
Techniques, pages 8–25
Materials, page 110
Suppliers, page 111

design decisions

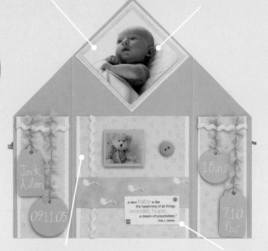

A black and white image looks wonderful with the blue and white colours of the card.

I cut the photo to a diamond shape so the cut-away card represented a baby's blanket. It also made a pleasant change to use a diamond-shaped photo.

The deckle-edged paper has the appearance of being frilly and the rickrack braiding is also associated with babies.

The rub-on alphabet and sentiments are easy to use and give the lettering a professional look.

deckle edge

I cut the circle-patterned blue paper with a deckle edge down each side for further embellishment. It also goes well with the ricrack braid.

continuous cut

Use a pair of large cutting scissors to obtain a neat continuous cut. The stopping and starting action of opening and closing smaller scissors may produce an uneven or jagged edge.

① Make the card using the large square of blue card following steps 1-2 on page 58 with the sides 7.5cm (3in) wide and the back 15cm (6in) wide. Measure and mark with a pencil 15cm (6in) across the top edge and the same down each side. Use a ruler and pencil to join each side mark to the top mark then cut along both lines. Put the removed card with the leftover pieces.

② Start the decorations by securing each of the blue strips onto a slightly larger white strip. Use alphabet rub-ons to create the baby's details on the smaller square of blue card. Cut each into a shape using the tag and circle dies. Punch a small hole in the top of the circles. Tie a blue fibre through each tag and twist together. Secure the tags with sticky fixer pads. Wrap white rickrack braid around each rectangle 1cm (³⁄₈in) from the top edge and glue to the back. Feed the fibres from the tags under and over the rickrack braid, twist together and trim.

Secure the large blue paper rectangle onto the slightly larger white paper. Wrap the long piece of rickrack braid around the card 1.5cm (⅝in) across from the left edge and glue to the back. Secure the strip of stork paper across the card 3.5cm (1½in) up from the bottom edge. Trim the border from the teddy photo sticker and secure on a leftover piece of blue card. Trim to a narrow border then secure in place with sticky fixer pads. Glue on the button. Rub a baby saying transfer onto white card, trim and secure using double-sided tape. Place on a cutting mat, make a small hole with the bradawl in opposite corners and add fancy brads.

fresh fonts

White rub-ons add a fresh look to the text. If you want to print your details from the computer then choose pale blue because you can't print in white.

Secure the square of blue patterned paper onto the slightly larger square of white card using double-sided tape. Secure the photo on top.

To decorate the card front lay the card blank out flat with the outside facing upwards. Use the stick provided to rub a transfer onto the bottom right and another to the top left.

Cut two 3 x 9.5cm (1½ x 3¾in) rectangles from leftover blue card and emboss. Trim to 2.5cm x 6.5 (1 x 2½in) and glue each one centrally on a 3.5cm (1⅜in) wide white rectangle. Lay the ribbon across the right card front and secure an embossed card over it so that its bottom edge is 10cm (4in) up from the bottom of the card and its side against the fold. Secure the second embossed card to the left card front using a ruler to help with alignment.

Add the inside decoration by turning the card over and using double-sided tape to secure the three decorated panels so that the bottom edges line up with the bottom of the card. Close the card and secure the baby photo at the top.

It's a tie

This card ties shut using a bow but a pretty buckle or 'D' rings secured to the ribbon would also work well.

This card can be shaped to suit the design or theme. Curve the front opening panels or reduce their height to bring more of the inside into the front design.

Full details of the papers and other decorative elements used to make the cards on these pages are provided on page 110.

forbidden corner

This is a terrific memento of a family fun visit and makes a really distinctive thank you card. With little pockets to store memorabilia such as tickets and extra photos it's almost a mini scrapbook.

Card size 26 x 28cm (10 ½ x 11in) folding down to 13 x 28cm (5¼ x 11in)

To avoid a symmetrical design I secured the decorated large tag to the left-hand front panel so that it was off centre and balanced it with stickers and buttons on the right.

Initially the co-ordinating alphabet stickers disappeared into the background paper. To give them more definition I randomly outlined the edges of each letter.

As the photos adorning this card are relatively small there are larger copies enclosed in a transparent memorabilia envelope along with a letter of thanks.

Here are just some of the items that you can pop into pockets. You could also include souvenirs such as pins, badges, erasers and pencils.

Printed twill goes well with the rustic design of the papers and adds texture. The buttons provide an extra design feature.

To accommodate the thickness of the pockets and to enable the card to close properly I added a double fold of 1cm (⅜in) to each side.

Little pockets enable entrance tickets and a scanned downsized copy of the brochure to be tucked inside. The shape of the pockets reflects the curve at the top. To give depth to the pockets they are secured with sticky fixer pads.

open house

Take a special photo of a friend's new home and use it to create a truly personal and unique card. This snapshot of the house as it is today will serve as a reminder in years to come when changes may have been made to the house and its surroundings.

Card size 30 x 26cm (12 x 10¼in) folding down to 15 x 26cm (6 x 10¼in)

On the card back is a pocket decorated with falling keys cut with a craft punch. When the large tag is in place, only the poem and not the sentiment can be seen (see page 21).

To create the appearance of a front door extra card is secured to the card front. Button snaps represent the doorknobs and I hung a bunch of keys (doll's house accessories) behind one. Embroidery silk (floss) wraps around the snaps, keeping the card closed.

I cut the card back into a roof shape then glued on alphabet scrabble tiles to spell out the sentiment.

The photo was taken especially for this card and is hung like a picture on a wall in keeping with the homely theme.

Keys punched from speckled patterned paper fall down each side panel. The specks of orange that look like rust lift the keys from the background.

Staying with the central rustic appearance both the side panels are decorated with plain twill overlapped with twill stickers that provide the sentiments. If preferred, you can rubber stamp the text.

The main decoration of this card is confined to the centre panel where rustic paper picks up the brickwork from the house in the photo. Wooden buttons and raffia complement the design.

birthday surprise

A pop-up card is enduringly popular, probably because it reminds us of our childhood days and the joy we felt when reading pop-up books. Perhaps because we associate it with our childhood it is particularly appropriate for a birthday card and may recall some of the excitement of earlier birthdays.

Many of us tend to look through the photos we already have when making a scrapbook card or page, but there is nothing to stop you arranging a mini photo shoot to obtain the ideal photo for your card. Here the children created a banner greeting on the computer and then printed it out. They were photographed holding it up and afterwards the banner was used at the birthday celebration.

When closed, the card is kept flat with the help of a ribbon tie. The vibrant wrap envelope was created using a plain sheet of co-ordinating paper. The front of the envelope is decorated with unused stickers (see the main picture) and leftover patterned paper extends the back top flap. For full details on making this type of envelope, see page 98.

Variations on the theme

For a get well soon, farewell or milestone birthday card organize a photo of your family/friends holding a shop-bought banner. Ask a friend to take a photo so that you can be included and arrange everyone in a line so the photograph is wide rather than tall. Alternatively, secure individual photos of people, animals or places on a photo mat to create the scene.

you will need

- ✓ Card maker's tool kit, page 8
- ✓ 11cm (4½in) coloured photo
- ✓ Red textured card
- ✓ 15 x 23cm (6 x 9in) card blank
  - 11 x 26cm (4¼ x 10¼in) strip
  - 12cm (4¾in) square
  - 18 x 10cm (7 x 4in) rectangle for a tag
  - Leftover piece
- ✓ Patterned paper
  - 22 x 14cm (8¾ x 5¾) rectangle with a design for the top (A)
  - 22 x 14cm (8¾ x 5¾) rectangle with a design for the bottom (B)
- ✓ 22 x 14cm (8¾ x 5¾) rectangle of plain paper
- ✓ Glitter stickers including 'Happy Birthday' motif
- ✓ Narrow green ribbon
  - 8cm (3in) length
  - 50cm (20in) length
- ✓ Craft punches
  - Circle 2.5cm (1in) diameter
  - Small hole

Card size 23 x 15cm (9 x 6in)

See also
Techniques, pages 8–25
Materials, page 110
Suppliers, page 111

design decisions

Glitter stickers are a quick way to fill in any gaps and add sparkle at the same time.

A tag in a pocket holds the greeting.

The photo is matted onto the same coloured card as the card blank, pulling design together.

The small parcels add further dimension to the layout and are easily secured by a small flap.

punch it

To position the punch perfectly on your paper, first cut a circle from scrap paper; fold in half from top to bottom, then from side to side and unfold. Place this template on the card, using the fold lines as guides, and draw an exact semicircle round the edge. Use this as your punching guide.

Decorate the inside by opening up the card and securing the top paper (A) centrally to the left-hand side with double-sided tape. Measure and mark 7cm (2¾in) down the right-hand side of the bottom paper (B), and punch a large semicircle at the mark (see the tip, left). Apply double-sided tape to the top, bottom and left-hand edge of the bottom paper and secure it centrally, as shown. This creates a pocket for the greetings tag.

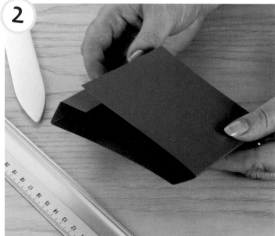

To add a pop up box, measure and score the 11 x 26cm (4¼ x 10¼in) strip of red card as shown in the diagram on page 109. Fold along each scored line then fold round to ensure that it fits together. Use double-sided tape to secure the overlap to the box side.

3

Apply double-sided tape to the box base and the box front and back sides. Only remove the backing tape from the box side to be secured to the top of the card. Open up the card and on the top edge of the card line up the box fold with the centre fold then press in place. Remove the backing paper from the box base then close the card to secure it.

4

Mount the photo centrally onto the 12cm (4¾in) square mat. Stick four parcels onto separate leftover pieces of card and score the card along the bottom of each parcel. Cut out, leaving a small flap at the base then taper the flap by cutting off the corners, as shown. On the red tag punch a hole halfway down one end, thread the short ribbon through it and trim the ends.

5

Remove the remaining backing tape from the box side and secure the photo mat in place so it is a little up from the bottom. (This ensures that the card will close easily.) Make sure that each parcel has space to lie flat when the card is closed then use double-sided tape to secure them in place. Finally add glitter stickers.

6

To decorate the card front stick the plain paper rectangle centrally on top. Secure the 'Happy Birthday' sticker onto leftover red card and trim around it. Lay it onto the card front to decide where to position it then determine where the centre of the card passes through it and mark with a pencil. Fold the long ribbon in half and secure it with a small piece of tape underneath so that a small loop protrudes at this point. Lay the 'Happy Birthday' card in place and add stickers around it. Secure it with sticky fixer pads, wrap the ribbon around the card, pass both ends through the loop and tie.

no peeking

Ensure that your pop-up doesn't poke out from inside the card and spoil the surprise. To do this, add the height of the photo mat to the width of the box top plus an allowance of 1cm (½in). For the pop-up to be enclosed this measurement must be less than the depth of the card.

double the fun

Give a staggered effect by using two smaller pop-up boxes of different widths side by side. For a stepped effect secure a shorter box to the front of a tall one. Stick a photo onto the tall one and journaling onto the smaller one.

Tidy view

Ensure that you only angle the presents a little otherwise you may see the flaps when the parcels are viewed from the front.

Happy Birthday Dad!

We had lots of fun taking this photo. Mum took lots but there was only this one of us both smiling at the same time!

We helped Mum make your card and envelope. Hope you like it.

Lots of Love Joshua and Sarah x x x x x x x x x

Taken on 22nd September 2005 for 25th September 2005.

Add your message to the tag – I wrote this one on a slightly smaller piece of yellow paper so it would stand out then fixed it on with double-sided tape. The ribbon tie on the tag helps draw attention to it when inside the pocket and makes it easier to pull out.

Full details of the papers and other decorative elements used to make the cards on these pages are provided on page 110.

You can add a pop-up box to most cards, irrespective of their shape and size. You can secure a photo or journaling to the pop-up and use two or more boxes to add dimension or create a scene. Before permanently securing the boxes, always double check that the pop-up won't protrude when the card is closed.

you're grand

This fun congratulations card takes its shape from a grand piano. Created in black for an authentic look, the white and red elements lift the card, giving it a bright and cheery feel.

Card size 22 x 15cm (8½ x 6in) opening to a height of 15cm (6in)

Crystal stickers co-ordinating with the piano keys provide the greeting on the top of the piano lid, and the sentiments and title inside.

Alter this to the shape of any items that open up. A bon voyage card could be made into a suitcase and a card in the shape of a computer would be amusing for a technical enthusiast.

The narrow frame around the photo echoes the bright red insert. On the inside of the piano lid more red is used for the punched musical notes and the backing of the crystal letters.

The shape of this card is bound to amuse and delight. The piano keys were taken from computer clip art but you could use a photocopy or draw your own with a black felt-tip pen.

The velveteen piano stool is secured to a strip of black card that slots into a pocket underneath the piano base. Pull it out to reveal the greeting.

Too much black made the card look sombre so to give it a lift I cut a smaller piano shape insert from red card (template on page 109) and secured it to the piano base. It also overlaps the edge of the piano keys, giving a neat appearance.

To complement the red musical notes, black ones are secured to the red piano insert. Small photographs of sheet music are also stuck to the insert but you could use shapes cut from music score patterned paper.

especially for you

The Victorian-style collaged papers used in this Christmas card send special wishes across the miles. It is a beautiful keepsake that contains personal message tags.

Card size 20 x 15cm (8 x 6in) opening to a height of 10cm (4in) with an 11cm (4½in) drop-down flap

I let the collage design on the main paper determine the overall effect of this card. Overlaying co-ordinating papers and stickers broke up the busy background and added further interest, pulling the colours together.

I like a little glitter at Christmas and when the design was complete I felt it lacked lustre. I enhanced each sticker with a little glitter glue to add a shimmer to the overall effect.

I tore the papers to produce a jagged white edge. This helps the papers blend together yet still retains some definition. If you have not tried creating a collage before then using a paper with a collage design will give you a head start.

The card flap is cut from the same card as the main card and is attached to it using two Sizzix die-cut card hinges. Note that these must be glued in place to work properly – the eyelets are purely a decorative element.

Although the Christmas messages were personal they did not need to be totally hidden from view. They are stored in a small wedding favour bag tucked behind a piece of toning ribbon. They are easily accessible and, if the recipient wanted, the bag could be removed without spoiling the card.

Mini tags are contained within a small wedding favour bag.

sweet sixteen

This spectacular zigzag card will amaze everyone that sees it. It may look complex but don't be fooled, the secret is in the measuring. It's a great card for a birthday because you can put a youthful picture on the left side, and a current picture on the right, as I did with Kate here. The two photos, although quite different, are complemented by the pastel colours and delicate patterns on the papers.

I used a range of papers that included a variety of tag stickers, and these encouraged me to experiment with the contemporary design on the insert. Instead of visible journaling, I decided to write mini cards onto which I matted the photos.

Off-cuts of card and paper plus unused tags and letters were used to make this attractive presentation box. It co-ordinates beautifully with the card and the matching gift tag. Both the card and tag can be stored safely within it. For full details on making this box, see page 102.

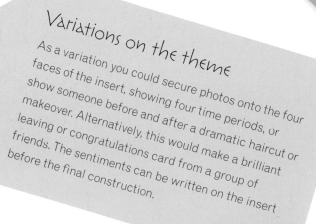

Variations on the theme

As a variation you could secure photos onto the four faces of the insert, showing four time periods, or show someone before and after a dramatic haircut or makeover. Alternatively, this would make a brilliant leaving or congratulations card from a group of friends. The sentiments can be written on the insert before the final construction.

you will need

- ✓ Card maker's tool kit, page 8
- ✓ Two coloured photos 4.5cm x 6.5cm (1¾ x 2½in)
- ✓ Peach textured card
  - 25 x 15cm (9¾ x 5¾in) rectangle
  - 24 x 15cm (9 ½ x 5¾in) rectangle
- ✓ Light green card
  - 28 x 9.5cm (11 x 3¾in) rectangle
  - Three 9 x 14cm (3½ x 5½in) rectangles
  - Two 7cm (2¾in) square top folding mini cards
- ✓ Small piece of pale blue card
- ✓ Three 8.5 x 13.5cm (3¼ x 5¼in) rectangles of floral paper
- ✓ Co-ordinating lined paper plus alphabet and tag stickers
- ✓ Pink three-dimensional paint
- ✓ 50cm (20in) length of thin white ribbon
- ✓ Small daisy craft punch
- ✓ Sizzix paddle punch – daisy (38-0832)
- ✓ Pastel sequins, needle and thread
- ✓ Two photo anchors and a slide mount
- ✓ Four different coloured eyelets
- ✓ Small hole punch and hammer
- ✓ Eyelet setting tool

See also
Techniques,
pages 8–25
Materials,
page 110
Suppliers,
page 111

**Card size 144cm x 10cm (17 x 8in) folded down to
10 x 20cm (4 x 8in)**

design decisions

The decoration on the card front states the greeting and introduces some of the design elements to be found inside.

The anchors are easily moved to reveal the journaling inside.

The daisy cut-outs in the insert allow the light to shine through from behind. The daisy theme is carried through the card, linking all areas together.

The unusual stickers encouraged the development of a contemporary design.

Photo anchors keep the small top-folding cards in place, giving a neat appearance.

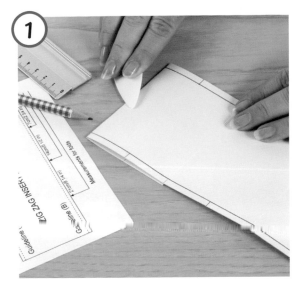

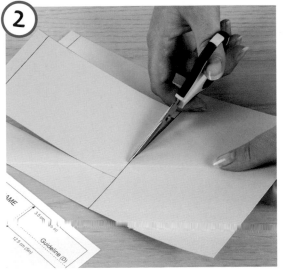

To make the insert, refer to diagram 1 on page 108 and measure 5mm ($^3/_{16}$in) from the top edge of the long green rectangle; draw guideline A. Repeat along the bottom edge to draw guideline B. From the right-hand side measure and mark each snip along guideline A. Use scissors to snip at each mark from the card edge to the guideline. Repeat along guideline B. Measure from the right-hand side to mark each fold. At each mark score from top to bottom with a stylus and ruler then crease well with a bone folder. Erase all pencil lines.

To make the outer frame, refer to diagram 2 on page 108. The larger peach rectangle is 1cm ($^3/_8$in) longer than the other to create an overlap for the tape so the two pieces can be joined. Measure 1cm ($^3/_8$in) from the right-hand side of the large peach card and draw a tape guideline from top to bottom. From the tape guideline measure 12.5cm (5in) and draw guideline C. Measure down guideline C and draw guideline D then measure up guideline C and draw a guideline E. Cut from the right-hand edge along these two guidelines then cut between them along C and remove the centre strip of card.

Use a pencil to draw all guidelines and make all marks as stated in each step. Keep them faint and easy to erase. Mine are drawn darker for photography.

making guides

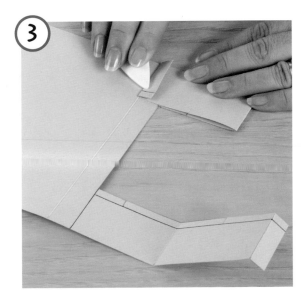

Referring to diagram 3 on page 108, measure 5mm ($^3/_{16}$in) out from both inner edges and draw guidelines F and G. From the tape guideline measure and mark the snips along guideline F then make the snips with scissors as before. From the tape guideline measure and mark each fold. At each mark score from top to bottom with a stylus and ruler then crease well with a bone folder. Finally score and fold along the tape guideline.

Take the shorter peach rectangle and repeat steps 2 and 3. This time there is no tape guideline and all measurements are made from the left-hand edge not the right.

zigzag template

Save time measuring by making a couple of templates for this card. Cut notches into the template to show the position of snips and folds and label each clearly.

dummy run

See how this card works by making one out of off-cuts and leaving on all your pencil marks. If it doesn't assemble then you can retrace your measurements to identify why.

Apply double-sided tape to the right side of both tape flaps and secure the second frame to the first. Before decorating check the insert fits by feeding it into the frame. The central fold on the insert points forwards and the central fold on the frame points backwards. Gently move the snips along so that they each interlock. Note that you will need to pull the frame outwards to accommodate the insert.

To decorate the insert first remove it from the frame and erase any remaining pencil marks and guidelines. Also erase any on the frame. Punch out daisy shapes from each face of the insert with the small craft punch and Sizzix paddle punch. Aim for a random effect. Also punch out extra daisies from the pale blue card and add centres to these and the green daisies with three-dimensional paint. Apply the stickers, glue on the daisies, and randomly sew on the pastel-coloured sequins with a needle and thread.

larger card

The instructions given are to create the card from readily available sheets of A4 (US letter) card. You can also make it by using a single sheet of A3 card. Firstly score and fold the card in half then omit steps 2 and 3 and make all measurements from the folded edge. Practice first using a sheet of inexpensive brown paper cut to size.

When decorating the frame first feed the insert back into the card so that you can get an overall feel for the design. On the first green rectangle secure a rectangle of floral paper centrally. Wrap round strips of lined paper from top to bottom and across the top. Enhance with alphabet stickers to create the greeting. Glue on two daisies, add a slide mount, decorate and secure with eyelets. Secure centrally to the back left of the frame (card front) with double-sided tape.

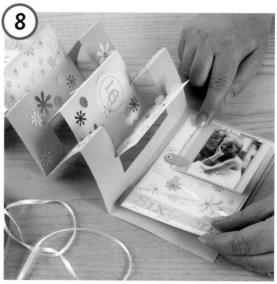

On the second rectangle secure the floral paper, wrap with ribbon and secure at the back with glue. Stick on the alphabet stickers, glue on the daisies and decorate one top-folding mini card by securing paper and the young girl's photo to the front. Secure the mini card then add a photo anchor to hold the card closed. Secure centrally to the front left with double-sided tape. Decorate the last rectangle with a similar design but this time use the current photo. Secure to the front right with double-sided tape.

The connected elements of this card mean that it works well as a suggested link between the years, people or places but experiment as there is scope for so much more.

Full details of the papers and other decorative elements used to make the cards on these pages are provided on page 110.

Across the miles

This delightful Christmas card is sure to be received with pleasure and can be displayed every year during the festive season.

Card size 53 x 20cm (21 x 8in) folded down to 12.5 x 20cm (4¾ x 8in)

When the card is closed, this face is on show, and should tie in with the decorations within.

I created the front decorations on a slightly smaller rectangle of blue card so that I could stitch on the snowflakes.

I found it easiest to place the sentiment and then decorate around it.

Instead of creating a presentation box this card could be tied closed with sheer white ribbon or wrapped in white tissue paper.

The photos are secured onto vellum tags edged with metal. I lifted the dull edges by painting them with glitter glue. Now the eye is drawn straight to the photos.

Single strands of silver embroidery silk (floss) wrapped around the photos and tags echo the glitter and holographic snowflakes, adding another texture and more sparkle.

Holographic snowflakes are secured by sewing a small white pearl seed bead through the centre. More beads are sprinkled over the vellum to give an impression of falling snow. These also hold the vellum in place.

Cool blue card and white vellum create an icy mood.

I trimmed the bottom-left photo so that it just focused on the group. To enable some of the pretty background to be included I tinted a copy of the photo in blue and then mounted the trimmed colour photo onto it.

In keeping with the two-colour theme I used white alphabet rub-ons to add the text and greetings.

To create a taller version I increased the amount of card at the bottom. As I kept the insert the same this then provided four larger areas for the greeting. Extra photos could also be secured here.

The mother took the two fun images of the family so she isn't present, and I added a separate picture of her that was taken at a different time. I placed it on the right of the card so that any discrepancy wasn't obvious.

friendship album

A true gift of love, this wonderful album makes a gorgeous parting gift for a good friend or neighbour. Comprising four pages, or boards, that are joined with twill tape, it can be hung up on display as a permanent reminder of friends from the past or folded up and stored safely. It is easily adaptable, so you can have more or less pages as desired, and you can add cards or pockets, as I did on the front, so you need never run out of space.

I had a single theme running across all the pages of this album, but if preferred you can use a mix-and-match selection of papers, choosing a different focal paper for each page but maintaining the overall continuity.

The cover is decorated with leftover papers and stickers in the same style as the four decorative boards. Notice how the ties cross the cover and make sure you are happy with the layout when they are in place.

Variations on the theme

Change these boards to relate to the four seasons in a year. This approach would be extremely effective for displaying photos taken, for example, in your garden or local park. The design would also make a very special Christmas album, incorporating memories of previous years. It would be a talking point for everyone to admire and reminisce over.

you will need

- ✓ Card maker's tool kit, page 8
- ✓ Coloured photos of various sizes
- ✓ Four 20 x 15cm (8 x 6in) rectangles of mount board or very thick card
- ✓ 14 x 10cm (5½ x 4in) rectangle of cream textured card
- ✓ Selection of collage and dictionary papers
- ✓ Sheet of patterned vellum
- ✓ Three-dimensional stickers
- ✓ Single circle closure
- ✓ Flat stickers and black alphabet stickers
- ✓ Tiny buttons or beads
- ✓ Embroidery silk (floss)
- ✓ Skeleton leaves
- ✓ Photo anchor
- ✓ Deckle-edged ruler (optional)
- ✓ Brown twill tape 1.5cm (½in) wide
  - Six 6cm (2¼in) strips
  - 1m (1yd) strip
  - 40cm (16in) strip
- ✓ Small hole punch and hammer

Album size 20 x 66cm (8 x 25½in) folded down to 20 x 15cm (8 x 6in)

See also
Techniques, pages 8–25
Materials, page 110
Suppliers, page 111

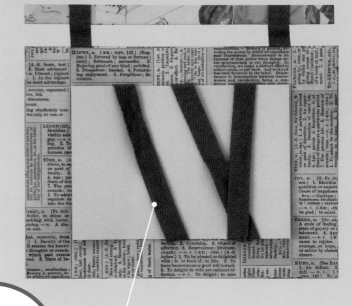

When the board is hanging up, wrap the closing ties around the cream card to keep them out of sight.

all change!

There are infinite possibilities to give this album a different look. You can change the size and shape of the boards and also the number you include.

To make each board, cut a rectangle 25 x 20cm (9½ x 7½in) from the collage paper. Lay the paper face down and secure the board centrally onto it using two strips of double-sided tape. Trim a triangle of paper from each corner, leaving a small amount of paper at the corner point to ensure an overlap. Secure each flap with double-sided tape.

Decorate the boards by wrapping and overlaying each one with torn paper and vellum strips. Secure these to the back with double-sided tape. Add the photos, stickers, buttons and any other decorations you like (see pages 84–85).

Link the boards together by laying two boards face down one above the other in order. On the bottom edge of the top board, measure and mark 3cm (1¼in) in from each side. Repeat for the top edge of the bottom board. Place the boards 1.5cm (⅝in) apart and join them by gluing two short lengths of twill tape to the back so that the outer edge of the tape touches the 3cm (1¼in) marks on the board. Repeat to join the other boards.

Cover the back of each board to give a neat appearance. To do this, cut a rectangle 19.5 x 14.5cm (7¾ x 5¾in) from the collage paper and use double-sided tape to secure it to the back of the board, as shown.

template trick

To help position the boards in step 3, cut a 20 x 1.5cm (8 x ⅝in) rectangle of scrap card and mark 3cm (1¼in) in from each end. Use this template to mark 3cm (1¼in) in from each side on the boards. Then place the template between the boards to automatically produce a gap of 1.5cm (⅝in).

Create the album wrap by laying 1m (1yd) of twill tape down the centre back of the bottom board. Glue the centre 5cm (2in) of tape to the board. Apply double-sided tape from top to bottom down the centre of the cream rectangle and 4cm (1½in) in from each short side. Secure centrally over the twill tape.

Add the hanging loop by marking 1cm (⅜in) down from the top edge and 1cm (⅜in) in from the right edge of the top board. Repeat for the top-left corner. Punch a hole where marked. Thread 40cm (16in) of twill tape through the holes from the back to the front. Double knot each end on the right side, trim at a slant then re-tighten the knots.

To decorate the front cover turn the album over and pull the hanging loop out of the way. Decorate the front cover in a similar theme to the boards, using torn papers, stickers and other leftover embellishments.

To close the album concertina fold the boards down and wrap the twill tape from the back cover around both sides to the front. Feed the tape under the hanging loop and tie loosely in a neat bow.

band aid

Instead of using a ribbon to tie the album closed try a card band. See the instructions on page 103 and make a narrow band based upon the outer cover of the presentation box. Ensure that it is large enough to fit over the closed album while still being tight enough to hold the pages securely.

design decisions

Full details of the papers and other decorative elements used to make this album are provided on page 110.

remember

The greeting dictated the order of my boards. If you do not use a greeting that spreads across the boards then arrange yours in a logical sequence, perhaps by date.

The flap at the top of the pocket holds the pictures securely when the album is folded down.

I wanted to create a backdrop that would be suitable for all the different photos. The collage design with torn edges and overlapping strips provides an interesting but not overpowering design.

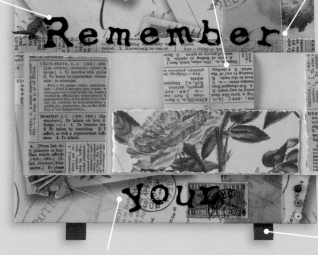

As I had lots of extra photos to include I added a front-opening card with a pocket inside. Photos from around the town and of memorable events are stored here

I chose black alphabet stickers so they would stand out clearly from the background paper. I tilted the letters to make it easier to align each one. The words link each board together as they spell out the sentiment.

Brown twill tape complements the colours in the papers and is more in keeping with the collage design than ribbon.

family

The file cover is held in place with a photo anchor and when opened a piece of co-ordinating paper unfolds. Here I have secured more photographs of the family but you could also use it for journaling.

This paper range includes three-dimensional stickers with sentiments. These pick up the colours from the papers and add dimension to the designs. You could make your own dimensional stickers by layering elements cut from the paper. Secure two or three layers together using sticky fixer pads.

This album could include photos of the family in their current home or photos of their house and garden.

I threaded small rustic beads onto strands of embroidery thread (floss) and secured three of these to the board so that they passed beneath the file. I also glued some extra beads around the layout.

friends

Vellum is wonderful for adding another texture to the composition. In this case it doesn't need to be secured at the front so just wrap it around the board and secure to the back with tape.

The card onto which the photo is matted has been secured at three sides to form a pocket for a tag.

Try looking for fun photos taken at parties or of the children in school plays or the day the family had a barbecue in the rain! Use technology to enhance an out-of-focus photo or zoom in on a face in the crowd.

Stamp stickers from the paper range reinforce the sentiment of keeping in touch with family and friends far away. Always try to include embellishments that link the boards together.

In this instance a recipe that is special to the couple in the photo is included. Personal sentiments can be written on the reverse of the tag.

neighbours

Sentiments are rubbed directly onto the photographs, adding a personal touch to each one.

I created a mini greeting card made from off-cuts of the papers so that a special memory or greeting could be recorded. It could even be used for the dog's paw print!

I opened up a small envelope, traced around it and created an open envelope for the mini card.

Small gold skeleton leaves picking up the theme from the photo are tucked behind some of the papers. Keep these in place with a spot of glue applied along the leaf's spine.

memory album

Recalling our fondest memories, an album is a wonderful way of preserving the joys of a life lived. Since this is an album you will want to put together with the utmost care, I recommend the Rollabind© system because it enables books to be created using your own choice of card or paper cut to any size. You can include as few or as many pages as you wish and the system enables you to insert or remove pages from anywhere in your book at any time. In essence it is completely adaptable.

My album is dedicated to the memory of my mother and I chose to keep it small and easy to handle. I used heritage papers and inserted vellum overlays to cover the designs. There is very little, if any, journaling on the pages as the information on family, friends, events and places is written separately within the book.

An album like this can grow over time as your memories come flooding back. And, because pages can be inserted anywhere, you can build up your album in any sequence.

Variations on the theme

Change the content completely and make a book all about you! Use it to display your interests, dreams, likes and dislikes, or just show one day in your life. Carry your camera everywhere and photograph everyday things that often get overlooked. Your cup of coffee, clothes on a washing line, the TV schedule and your nightdress! Imagine looking back on it in ten years time – what a wonderful piece of history.

1960

1970

1980

1990

2000

you will need

✓ Card maker's tool kit, page 8
✓ Rollabind© kit and eight small rings
✓ Black and white photos
✓ Colour photos
✓ Black card
  • Two 20cm (8in) squares (front & back covers)
  • Leftover pieces
✓ Eight 19.8 x 20cm ($7^7/_8$ x 8in) card rectangles in various colours (dividers)
✓ 17.5 x 20cm (7 x 8in) card rectangles in various colours (pages)
✓ 17.5 x 20cm (7 x 8in) vellum rectangles (for the overlays)
✓ Selection of patterned papers
✓ Metal embellishments, alphabet and numbers
✓ Selection of ribbons
✓ Small square craft punch
✓ Use of a computer and printer or rubber stamps or rub-on letters

Album size 20cm (8in) square

See also
Techniques, pages 8–25
Materials, page 110
Suppliers, page 111

Choose papers that suit the mood you wish to create. This paper reminded me of traditional wallpaper and sets a nostalgic note.

central titles

Take the hassle out of calculating where to secure the letters for the title names. Glue the letters onto a long card strip so that they are around the middle. When complete get them exactly central following the instructions on page 18.

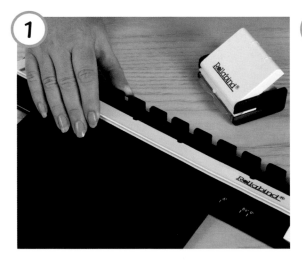

To make the front cover, lift the magnetic paper holder and slide one black cover under it. Line up the top edge with the 15cm (6in) mark and ensure that one side edge is butted up against the 'line up rule'. Press the paper holder back down.

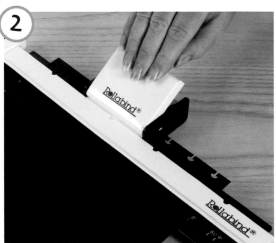

Swing the 'line up rule' underneath the paper guide tray, leaving the binding edge of paper extended out beyond the paper guide. Line up the punch on the exposed paper so that its notch fits into the notch on the magnet holder and punch. Repeat along the edge.

3

To decorate the cover, secure patterned paper down the centre. Build up the remaining design on a smaller piece of black card using decorative paper and metal embellishments. Secure centrally down the front using double-sided tape.

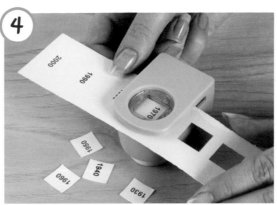

4

For the dividers type eight relevant dates, print out onto cream card and then punch each one into a square using the craft punch. Alternatively use rubber stamps or rub-on letters.

great gift

Use the Rollabind© system to create an album as a special gift. Send individual pages to family members and friends to decorate and then assemble.

5

Repeat steps 1 and 2 on the divider cards then score 2.5cm (1in) from each right-hand edge. Refer to the table right to create the tabs. Referring to column A, measure down from the top and remove the excess card from below, up to the scored line. Referring to column B, measure down from the top and remove the excess card from above, up to the scored line. Add dates to the tabs.

6

To make the back cover take the remaining black square card and repeat steps 1 and 2. Slip the black and gunmetal rings into the notches on the back cover and then build up the album by adding first the dividers and then the front cover.

	A	B	date
1	2.5cm (1in)	Zero	1930
2	5cm (2in)	2.5cm (1in)	1940
3	7.5cm (3in)	5cm (2in)	1950
4	10cm (4in)	7.5cm (3in)	1960
5	12.5cm (5in)	10cm (4in)	1970
6	15cm (6in)	12.5cm (5in)	1980
7	17.5cm (7in)	15cm (6in)	1990
8	Zero	17.5cm (7in)	2000

Use the table above to create the tabs on the divider cards (see step 5).

7

Create the scrapbook pages using the narrower card. For each one repeat steps 1 and 2 then add photos, papers, metal embellishments and ribbon (see pages 90–91).

8

To protect the scrapbook pages add a vellum overlay for each one. Using the vellum, repeat steps 1 and 2 then add to the album so that each one lies on top of a scrapbook page.

fancy vellum

Ring the changes by using coloured or patterned vellum for the overlays.

This album is separated by dividers into groups of ten years, so where an exact date is not known the scrapbook page can be added to the most appropriate year block.

childhood days

These two photos were taken in the same place, approximately six months apart. I felt that they complemented each other and so put them together on a single page.

As the photos were a little out of focus I enhanced them using photographic software on the computer. Professional photographers can repair torn and damaged photos and enhance blurred or faded ones.

I arranged the photos off-centre so that there would be one larger space to use for embellishments.

The photographs are secured using clear photo corners so when I am able to find out the year they were taken I can update my copies.

These papers are copies of fabric and the checked pattern was not quite square. To take the eye away from the discrepancy at the edges I trimmed them with a deckle-edge blade.

Before printing my photos I typed in the children's names. I rotated the text and moved it into position alongside each child.

Create your layout first and move it around before securing it. Now if you want to fold ribbon behind the backing paper you won't have to prise it off with a craft knife!

fifties belle

The patterned paper reminded me of wallpaper from many years ago so I based this layout around a photo hanging on the wall.

I chose metal accents throughout the album and here decorative photo corners add definition to the outer photo mat.

Only the year the photo was taken is known. It was not essential to add in the century but making the number four digits gave it more impact.

When I placed the metal charmed phrase and date directly onto the patterned paper they were lost so I matted them onto blue card.

Two ribbon charms are glued above the photo and the smaller photo mat is secured to the ribbon so that it can be lifted to reveal journaling.

The easiest way to secure the ribbon hanging is to thread ribbon through the charms and glue in place on the page. Apply double-sided tape to a small piece of card and press the ribbon on top. Apply a second strip of double-sided tape over the ribbon and onto the small piece of card then secure the photo mat in place. This also gives a neat appearance to the back.

wonderful wedding

I incorporated two metal photo flips to hold the photo mat in place, which can be lifted to view journaling or another photo.

The photo was taken so that half a handbag was in view! I covered it with three short lengths of sheer ribbon topped with a metal flower. It hides the bag and adds a decorative element.

The pretty floral paper is excellent for the backing as it picks up the colours in both the pink and green outfits.

There is more pink than green in the paper so I chose to mount the paper onto a complementary plain green card.

Measure and mark with a pencil the position of each photo flip. Lay each one in place at the pencil mark and press hard to make an impression. Remove then punch the hole and set the flip with an eyelet setter and hammer. Lay the mat in place and repeat the process to secure the top of each flip.

As the exact date of this photo is known, it is stated using alphabet charms mounted on a strip of green card.

The ribbon under the metal flower is picked up here by running a length across the paper underneath the date.

cheers!

I decided to create a frame on this page so I secured the patterned paper an equal distance from the right side, the top and the bottom edge.

Make a hole in each corner for the brads using a template to ensure that each is the same distance from the corner. Apply a little 'dry' glue, such as Studio Tac, over the holes and then secure the ribbon. Push the brads through the holes and open up the wings.

The sheer ribbon that frames the photo and overlays the paper softens the bold pattern.

It appears that the paper is just held in place with the metal brads but the paper was first secured with double-sided tape.

Although taken in the eighties the exact date and place of the photo is unlikely ever to be known so the journaling is restricted to who is in the photograph.

The ribbon immediately under the photo is the same distance away from it as the ribbon at the sides are away from the edges for symmetry.

let's ski album

Ever had lots of photographs on a single subject and wanted to use them all? They might come from a fantastic holiday, a close friend's wedding, special birthday, school play or particular activity. Now you can present them all in this simple but spectacular mini album that you can make yourself. The pages are glued together accordion style, enabling you to display all of them at once, and you can add as many pages as you like before you attach the covers.

Because of the way this album is constructed the pages will be seen as a whole, so you need to think of the decorations accordingly. You could have a continuous background across all the pages as I did for the skiing album, or link each page by using similar colours, patterns or photographs. Another idea is to use a time or dateline running across the album as you show changes over time – the development of a child from birth to adulthood or the progress of an event, perhaps including getting dressed for a party, arriving, the celebrations and the aftermath.

This mini album is great for displaying and storing holiday memories. There's space for lots of photos and plenty of additional interest provided by the use of textured papers. You can stand it up to reveal all the images at once or fold it closed and secure it with the ribbon tie for safety, as shown here.

variations on the theme
The snowy background on this album is ideal for displaying your skiing holiday photos, but it's easily adapted for other occasions. Use strips of yellow velveteen paper for a beach holiday, for example, or add rolling green hills for a stay in the country.

you will need

- ✓ Card maker's tool kit, page 8
- ✓ Blue paper or card:
  - 20cm (8in) square
  - three 21 x 20cm (8¼ x 8in) rectangles for the main pages
  - 19 x 7cm (7½ x 2¾in) rectangle for a pocket
- ✓ Two 18cm (7in) squares of striped paper to decorate the covers
- ✓ Four 20cm (8in) squares of glittered angel hair
- ✓ Three 20 x 16cm (8 x 6¼in) rectangles of white velveteen paper
- ✓ Two 21cm (8¼in) squares of mount board
- ✓ Two 24cm (9½in) squares of white paper
- ✓ 14 x 17cm (5½ x 6¾in) white card blank
- ✓ Scrap bits of white, orange, purple and yellow card
- ✓ Snowflake buttons
- ✓ Acrylic tags and small silver brads
- ✓ Crystal alphabet stickers
- ✓ White fibre
- ✓ 120cm (1½yd) of 1.5cm (⅝in) wide white organza ribbon and three white pony beads
- ✓ Circle craft punches, 2.5cm (1in) and 1.5cm (⅝in) diameter

Album size 21cm (8¼in) square

See also
Techniques, pages 8–25
Materials, page 110
Suppliers, page 111

The white velveteen paper with its tactile surface makes superb snow.

glue know-how

When gluing two pieces of card together, start pressing the join at the centre and move outwards towards each edge to help ensure that the pieces stay put. Hold in place for a minute while the glue dries. If preferred, use double-sided tape but make the joining flap a little wider than the tape. Note that, unlike when using glue, once in place the flap cannot be adjusted.

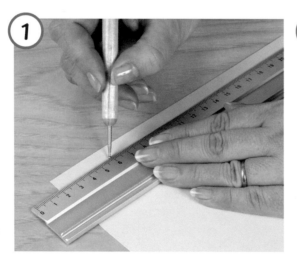

To make the pages, measure, score and fold 1cm (⅜in) in along the longer side of each large blue rectangle. This creates a small flap that will be used to join the pages together.

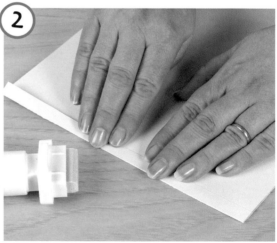

During assembly keep the flaps on the left. Lay out the first rectangle with its right side up and apply glue along the flap up to the scored line. Lay the blue square on top with its right side facing down. Line up the top, bottom and right-hand edges and ensure that the left-hand side is butted against the scored line. Secure the flap by pressing it down on the paper. Use this method to secure the second blue rectangle to the first and the third blue rectangle to the second. You now have four square album pages.

3

Along the top and 16cm (6¼in) down each side of the first three pages apply Studio Tac adhesive tape. Secure one rectangle of angel hair onto each page. On the last page, apply the adhesive to all four edges and secure the square of angel hair, then create a pocket by securing the small blue rectangle along the bottom using sticky fixer pads.

4

Cut out the velveteen paper in the shape of a snowy landscape and lay it on the pages (see the tip, right). Do not allow it to overlap or butt up to the folds or it will stop the pages closing properly; trim as necessary then glue the paper in place, starting with the first page.

snow template

Use scrap paper to make templates for your snowy landscape, which runs over three pages of the album. This will ensure that you don't make any mistakes with your velveteen paper

5

Decorate the pages and apply your photographs, using your own ideas or following my layout as shown on pages 96–97.

6

To make the covers, apply double-sided tape along each edge of each mount board square and secure centrally on a white paper square. Cut away a triangle at each corner (do not trim right up against the corner). Stick in place.

tidy up

After you have secured each flap press the small amount of excess paper at the corner flat with a bone folder or your finger nail for a clean finish.

7

To assemble, glue the back of the first and final pages centrally to one cover each. Glue a striped paper square onto the front cover and concertina fold the album shut. Fold the ribbon in half, crease and open. Lay the ribbon halfway down the back cover with the fold at the 'spine' and stick the second striped square onto the cover, trapping it in place. Glue a little of the ribbon to the back cover.

8

Decorate the front cover. Cut both ends of the ribbon to a slant and thread one pony bead onto both. Next thread one pony bead onto each single ribbon and knot each end. To close the album, slide the nearest bead towards it, and to open it slide the bead away from it.

cover story

To decorate the front cover, I used the same buttons and crystal stickers that I had used on the album pages.

design decisions

Arrange the pictures to tell a story or in a way that is clear for the viewer. I devoted a page to each child, bringing in mum and dad at the end.

Use sticky fixer pads to secure some of the photographs so that they are raised off the page. This gives them greater emphasis.

Embellish the folds, if desired. This adds another dimension and covers the joins in the white velveteen paper. I used a length of white fibre for this, tied near the top.

Clear acrylic tags continue the icy theme. I placed a tag over each of the small photographs and over the date, checking them for fit first and trimming away the excess. Each tag is secured with a silver brad – you'll need to make a small hole in the page first with a bradawl before you can insert these. Notice how the tags have a slight magnifying effect.

Punched circles of card make an excellent background for the words, drawing attention to them, providing a stylish lift and adding colour to the page. Punch the circles first from blue or white card and attach one alphabet sticker onto each one to make up the titles. Then position the words on the pages and glue in place.

Angel hair is a translucent paper with fine fibres trapped inside. It comes in several colours including white. The fine glittery paper used here allows the blue paper underneath to show through but gives it a glittering, shimmering finish that helps to capture the frosty sparkle in the air.

Fill any large gaps with buttons or other embellishments that enhance your theme. When using buttons, cut off the shanks and stick in place with glue dots.

LA PLAGNE

JAN 2006

The fallen snow, cut from white velveteen paper, gives continuity to the first three pages as well as providing an additional texture.

This card sits in the pocket on the final page of the album and features a pretty photo of the village, which is still in view when the card is in place. The additional space on the card can be used for journaling, additional photos or holiday memorabilia such as tickets and maps. Because this part of the card is out of sight when the card is in the pocket, it would be a good place to put a humorous photo, perhaps one that only the select few will be allowed to view.

envelopes and boxes

Now that you've made your card, you'll need something to put it in for presentation purposes. If you are going to give your card by hand, the envelope or box can be as decorative as you like, but if it's going through the post, make sure it is sturdy and has a label or undecorated area for the address. Instructions are given here for two types of envelope and a simple presentation box to get you started.

To protect your photographs properly, I would recommend using acid-free products for the envelope or box, especially if the recipient is likely to store the card inside. If this isn't necessary then you have a wider range of papers to choose from. Try using wrapping paper, brown paper, (plain or decorated with a stamped design) and wallpaper.

first glance

The envelope is important for first impressions, so allow the time to make something stylish.

I had insufficient paper for the Birthday Surprise (page 68) envelope, but I turned necessity to my advantage and added a top flap using a piece of co-ordinating paper.

The pretty envelope above, which was made to fit the thank you card on page 56, closes with sheer ribbon threaded through holes in the top and bottom flaps. The area around the holes is reinforced with a little card to help prevent the paper tearing.

It's a wrap

The easiest way to create an envelope is to wrap the card like a present and deliver it by hand. You'll need paper that is 2½ times as wide as the shortest measurement of the card. If you can't get this then try a two-piece envelope (page 100).

you will need

✓ Card maker's tool kit, page 8
✓ Paper (see step 1 for size)

See also
Protecting your creations, page 10

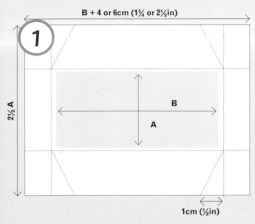

(1)

On a scrap of paper draw a plan of your envelope to calculate how much paper is required. Measure your card and multiply the shorter length (A) by two and a half as shown in the diagram above. If you card is quite flat add 4cm (1¾in) to the longer length (B) or if it is bulky add 6cm (2½in).

(2)

Lay the card in the middle of the paper, as shown. Fold the paper across one long edge of the card and crease with a bone folder then repeat for the other long edge. Open the paper out and repeat this process for the two shorter edges.

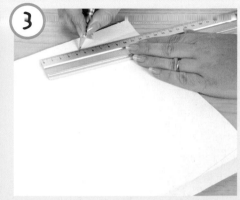

(3)

On each shorter side cut from the outside edge along the two creases, stopping at the point where two creases cross. Measure and mark with a pencil 1cm (½in) inwards from each of the uncut creases then draw a pencil guideline from this mark to the nearest cut.

(4)

Remove the corners by cutting down each pencil line then along the fold to the edge, as shown.

(5)

Re-wrap the card and secure the top flap with a little glue. Alternatively, use ribbon to wrap the envelope like a gift.

quicker wrap

The angled line marked in step 3 gives a decorative angled edge but for speed simply remove each corner by cutting along the folds.

Two-piece envelope

I based this design on a coin envelope because I wanted the card to be completely enclosed so that there wasn't any possibility of glue from the flap getting onto the card. This design is suitable for posting but do ensure that you make it from a good weight paper so that it is robust.

you will need

✓ Card maker's tool kit, page 8
✓ Paper (see step 1 for size)

See also
Protecting your creations, page 10

This envelope was used for the birth announcement card shown on page 62. The paper was only just deep enough for the card so I wasn't able to add an overlap for double-sided tape along the bottom edge. To get around this I scored a strip of card down the middle, folded it over the bottom opening and secured it to the front and back with double-sided tape.

Whoever would have thought of making a see-through envelope? It might not be your first thought, but it works very well, enabling the recipient to have an enticing glimpse of the card within.

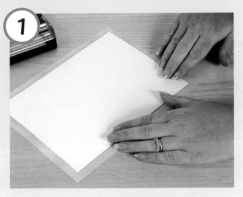

To create the envelope back panel measure the width of the card and add 2cm (¾in) for a flat card or 3cm (1¼in) for a bulkier one. Measure the height of the card and add the same additional amount. Cut the paper to this size.

Create the envelope front by cutting the paper so it is at least 3cm (1¼in) wider than the back panel and at least 6cm (2½in) taller. Secure double-sided tape along the bottom of the paper then fold it up along the edge of the tape and crease well. Place the back panel face down centrally on the front piece, lining it up with the crease at the bottom. Draw down both edges and mark the two top corners, as shown.

Stick double-sided tape along each edge. Use the pencil line as a guide and leave just a fraction between it and the edge of the tape. Measure between the top two corners, halve to find the mid point and mark with a pencil. From this point measure up and mark at least 5cm (2in) away. Use a pencil to draw a line out from this mark through one of the top corners and continue it over the double-sided tape. Repeat on the other side.

hidden inside

Laying your back panel face down ensures that if your pencil slips as you are tracing then the marks are on the inside and hidden from view.

easy sticking

When securing long lengths of double-sided tape, cut a strip from the roll and then secure it starting from the middle and working out to each end.

Cut along the two top pencil lines and then trim the excess paper away from the sides along the outer edge of the double-sided tape. Fold up the bottom edge and mark where the tape touches the outer edge of the tape on the sides. Open up then fold in each side, creasing well and marking where this tape touches the tape at the bottom. Draw a line across the bottom corners to join up the two marks. Trim the excess from the corners using the line as a guide but keeping 2mm (¹⁄₁₆in) away from it so there will be a small overlap at the corners.

Lay the back panel right-side up on the front piece within the pencil lines. Fold up the bottom edge, adjust the panels as necessary then remove the protective tape strips and secure. Repeat for both sides, as shown.

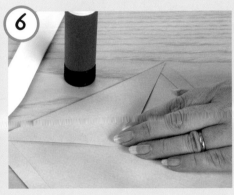

Erase any pencil lines from the top flap, place your card in the envelope, fold down the flap and glue closed.

outside overlaps

When adapting this envelope to your own measurements always ensure that you keep the overlapped edges on the outside. If they are inside you may find that your card gets caught on them.

Presentation box

I based this design on a matchbox because it is simple but effective. It's exciting as the recipient slides out the drawer to reveal the card hidden inside! If you intend to post the card, make the box from heavyweight card to protect all your hard work.

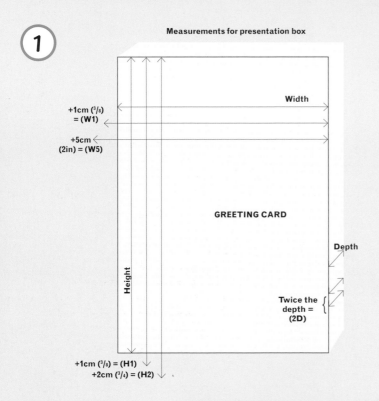

Measurements for presentation box

+1cm (³⁄₈) = (W1)
+5cm (2in) = (W5)
Width
GREETING CARD
Height
Depth
Twice the depth = (2D)
+1cm (³⁄₈) = (H1)
+2cm (³⁄₄) = (H2)

To create the inner tray first calculate its dimensions. Referring to the diagram shown above and to the abbreviations in the chart, right, write the measurement down against each letter so you can refer to it easily. Measure the width and the height of the card then hold the card so it is relatively flat, but not squashed, and measure the depth.

Calculating the dimensions	
D1	*the depth + 1cm (³⁄₈in)*
2D1	*D1 x 2*
W1	*the width + 1cm (³⁄₈in)*
W5	*the width + 5cm (2in)*
H1	*the height + 1cm (³⁄₈in)*
H2	*the height + 2cm (³⁄₄in)*

Cut the box base card to W1 + 2D1 by H1 + 2D1. Place it on the cutting mat and measure and mark with a pencil D1 in from each edge. Use a ruler and stylus to score along the marked lines.

Along one long side measure 1cm (³⁄₈in) into one of the corner squares. Draw a guideline from this mark to where two scored lines cross. Cut up this line then carefully cut up the adjacent scored line and remove a triangle of card from the corner square. Repeat for the other corners.

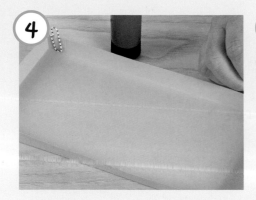

4 Use a bone folder to crease well along each scored line. Fold up two adjacent sides and apply glue to the underside of the corner piece. Fold inwards and press into place on the adjacent side. Use a paperclip to clamp the card together while the glue dries. Repeat on the remaining corners.

5 **For the outer cover** cut one piece of card H2 high and W5 + 2D1 wide. Measure in from the left side 1.5cm (⅝in), score and fold over. This creates a flap for the double-sided tape. Lay the box base against the fold and mark about 2mm (1/16in) away from the top edge on the cover.

6 Score along this mark and fold over. Lay the box base against the second crease and mark a fraction away from the edge on the cover. Score along this mark and fold over. Open out the cover then bend it gently over to line up the second fold with the third. Mark where the first fold touches the green card. Score along this mark and fold over. You now have five panels: a flap, a side, the base, a side and a flap.

7 Secure double-sided tape down the outside of the first and fourth creases then trim away any excess card.

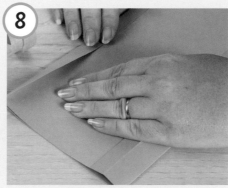

8 **For the back panel** cut one piece of card to H2 high and the width of the large centre panel on the outer cover. Remove the backing tape from the cover, butt the panel up to the fold and press firmly. Repeat for the other side.

allowance

If you make the outer cover to exactly the same width and depth as the box tray it will be too tight. Allowing the fraction extra when measuring the cover in step 6 should give a good, but not too tight fit.

using glue

Instead of double-sided tape you can use glue to secure the back panel to the outer cover, holding it firmly in place for a few minutes while the glue dries.

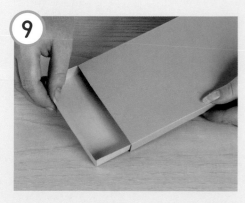

9 Put the card in the box base and feed this into the box cover.

This box holds the Sweet Sixteen birthday card featured on page 74. Decorated in the same papers as the card, it is a lovely box that the recipient will wish to save with the card.

from cards to pages

Sometimes your pictures will be so good and you'll like a layout so much that you want to keep a copy for yourself. You can, of course, simply make a second card to store away, but a much better idea is to make a scrapbook page based on the card design. Once in the album the page will be protected and you can easily find it and share it around.

Here are two examples of cards that I've adapted to suit 12 x 12in scrapbook pages. Every design is different, so there are no hard and fast rules on how to make the transfer from card to page, but these samples should give you some ideas and show how easy it can be. Further design ideas for scrapbooks are given on the following pages.

sk8erboy

I found the paper used on this scrapbook page when I was designing the card. I cut out sections of the paper for the card, but for the scrapbook page I was able to use the whole sheet.

This thank you card for a great skateboard has bold words running across and down the page (see page 36). The card is basically black and grey on a red background, while the scrapbook equivalent is designed the other way around with red on black and grey.

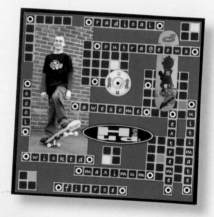

I used the full sheet of patterned paper as the background.

I kept to the style of the card by using strips of red card to overlay the patterned paper both vertically and horizontally.

Careful placement of the card strips, photos and text ensures that many of the words on the background paper are visible.

The funky title is a play on text messaging shorthand and is perfect for the young, contemporary design.

In keeping with the bold colour scheme of red and black I printed the journaling in black on red card. I then matted this onto black card to lift it from the background.

Easter message

You might not think that a panoramic card would translate very easily into a square format, but this layout actually came together quite easily. Dividing the page horizontally provides a change of pace from the other scrapbook pages.

The original card (see page 42) has a very different format but the overall design of the scrapbook page, shown below, feels the same.

This would make a delightful framed picture. Take a box frame and create an Easter-themed design with plenty of depth. Use the same papers and ideas but also incorporate silk butterflies, dried flowers and a textured paper for the grass.

I decoupaged the complete blooms and the butterfly's wings.

With more space to play with I increased the size of the original rabbit photo while still keeping the slim white border.

I wanted to be able to give an impression of the rabbit's size, include the surrounding greenery and show what the weather was like on the day the photo was taken. To achieve this I chose a second image of the rabbit and positioned it so the rabbit is looking over towards the centre of the page.

The green ribbon is secured across the top of the page and also over the join between the paper and the pocket. It diverts the eye from any discrepancy in the pattern matching.

I did not want the end of the tag sticking out from the edge of the page so I reduced the length of the pocket by 8cm (3in).

The journaling is written on a tag in a similar way to the card. To create a hidden pocket I secured a rectangle with the identical pattern to the bottom of the page. This produces an almost seamless effect.

scrapbook layouts

If you are suffering from creative block use one of these layouts as a springboard to get your creative juices flowing again. Just as the card designs can be translated into scrapbook pages, these layouts can be used to inspire your cards, whatever their format.

Here are ten layouts for one, two, three or more photos. Some designs are simple while others are a little more intricate and you can easily alter them by adding or removing different elements. As you may need to play around with the design so that it fits your requirements I suggest you start with a rough sketch. Draw a large square on a piece of scrap paper and sketch out the layout within it. Add your title and decide upon the areas that you want to fill with embellishments and journaling.

When you are happy with your plan either use it as a guide to create your page or redraw it to include exact measurements. Keep in mind that this is just a guide and that as you start creating you will probably find that it evolves further.

Create a background using a shape taken from the photograph. Try any simple shape such as a computer, house, gift box, Easter egg or beach ball.

Lay irregular widths of paper or card over the background to pick up two colours from a photo – it's both quick and easy.

Secure the photo off-centre then balance the design by dividing the background into rectangles.

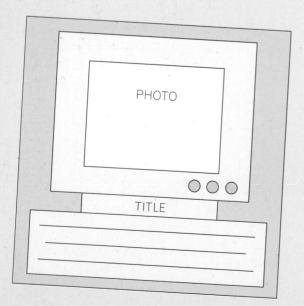

Soften a geometric design by using a craft punch to round the corners of the backing papers. Try decorative corner punches for a feminine effect.

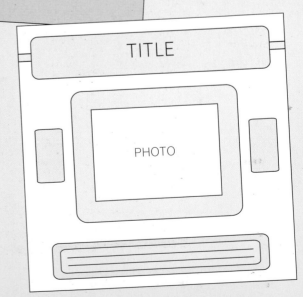

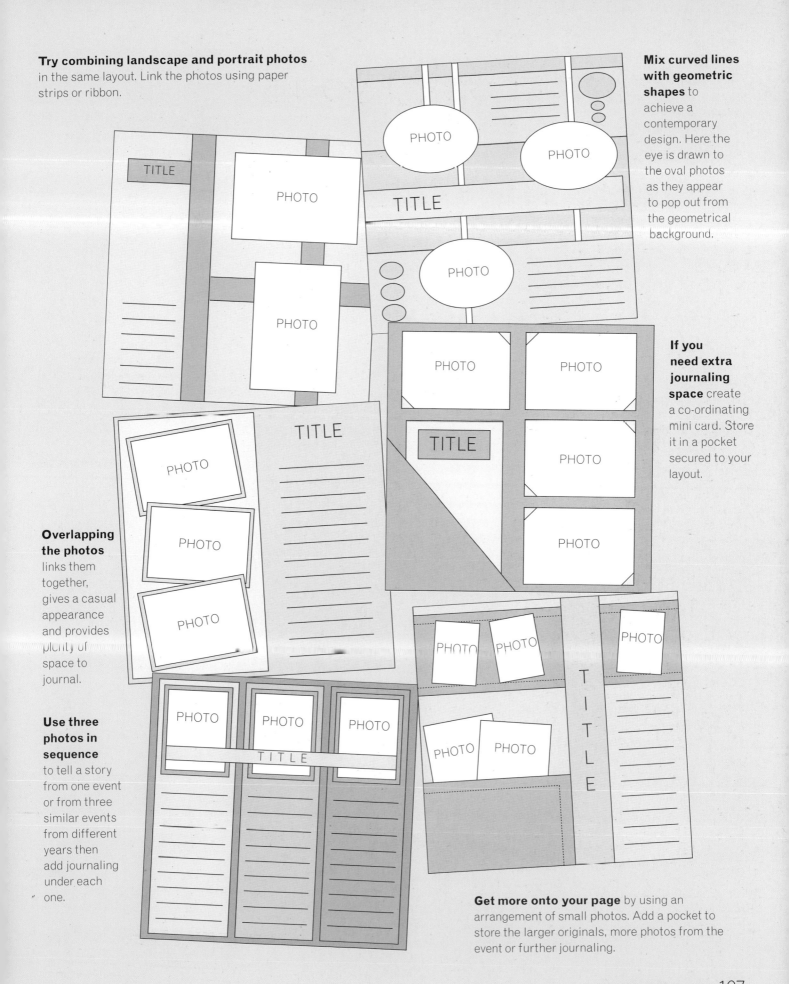

Try combining landscape and portrait photos in the same layout. Link the photos using paper strips or ribbon.

TITLE

PHOTO

PHOTO

Mix curved lines with geometric shapes to achieve a contemporary design. Here the eye is drawn to the oval photos as they appear to pop out from the geometrical background.

PHOTO

PHOTO

TITLE

PHOTO

If you need extra journaling space create a co-ordinating mini card. Store it in a pocket secured to your layout.

PHOTO

PHOTO

TITLE

PHOTO

PHOTO

TITLE

PHOTO

PHOTO

PHOTO

Overlapping the photos links them together, gives a casual appearance and provides plenty of space to journal.

PHOTO

PHOTO

PHOTO

PHOTO

PHOTO

PHOTO

TITLE

PHOTO

PHOTO

Use three photos in sequence to tell a story from one event or from three similar events from different years then add journaling under each one.

PHOTO

PHOTO

PHOTO

TITLE

Get more onto your page by using an arrangement of small photos. Add a pocket to store the larger originals, more photos from the event or further journaling.

Diagrams and templates

**Sweet Sixteen
(page 74)**

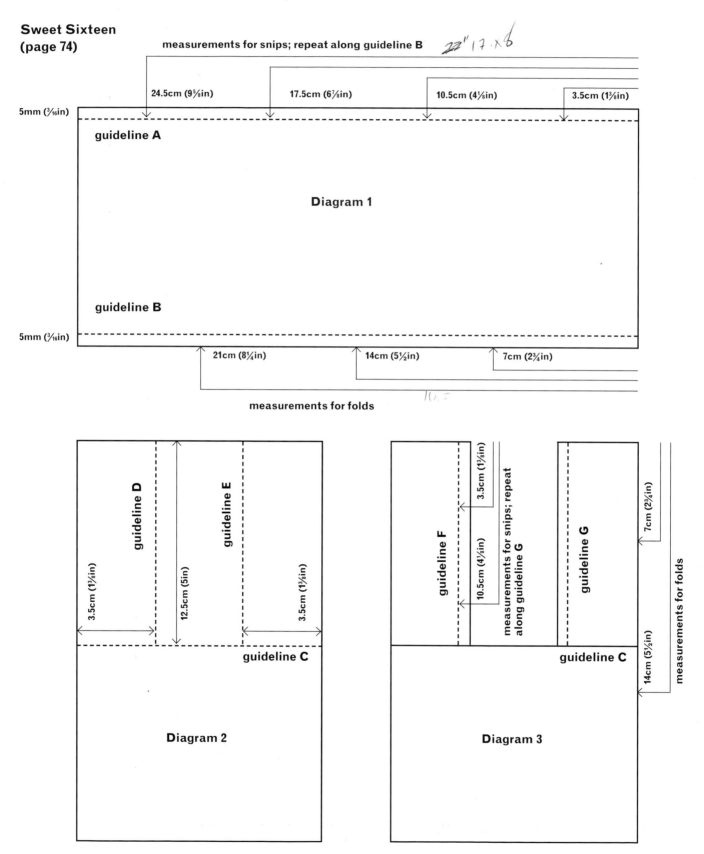

measurements for snips; repeat along guideline B   22" 17 . x 6

| 24.5cm (9⅝in) | 17.5cm (6⅞in) | 10.5cm (4⅛in) | 3.5cm (1⅜in) |

5mm (³⁄₁₆in)

guideline A

Diagram 1

guideline B

5mm (³⁄₁₆in)

| 21cm (8¼in) | 14cm (5½in) | 7cm (2¾in) |

measurements for folds   16.5

Diagram 2

guideline D

guideline E

3.5cm (1⅜in)   12.5cm (5in)   3.5cm (1⅜in)

guideline C

Diagram 3

guideline F

3.5cm (1⅜in)

10.5cm (4⅛in)

measurements for snips; repeat along guideline G

guideline G

7cm (2¾in)

measurements for folds

guideline C

14cm (5½in)

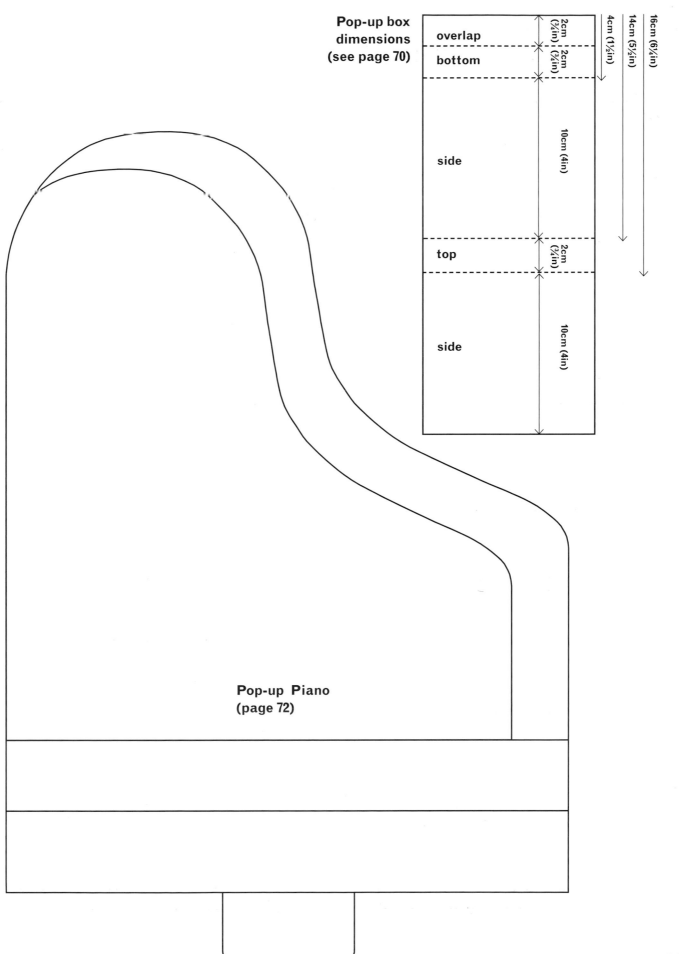

Pop-up box dimensions (see page 70)

overlap	2cm (¾in)
bottom	2cm (¾in)
side	10cm (4in)
top	2cm (¾in)
side	10cm (4in)

4cm (1½in)

14cm (5½in)

16cm (6¼in)

Pop-up Piano (page 72)

Materials

Scrapbooking and card-making materials are an ever-changing field so you may not be able to get exactly the items I used – you may even find better ones. However, because it is helpful to know where materials come from, I have listed the papers I used in my main cards and variations along with any items that are a little bit different.

Page 26, Look who's 40!
Metal tag by Making Memories

Page 30, New Birth – kids 8 x 8in paper pack (HOTP 5202) from Hot Off The Press

Page 30, Birthday Friendship – paper by PSX

Page 31, Green for Go – mixing bright papers (HOTP 3256) by Hot Off The Press

Page 32, Family Christmas – Christmas ice tiles (952) by Ki Memories, Christmas candy (322) and holly jolly dotted line (321) papers by Doodlebug Design Inc

Page 36, Great Skate – tough talk (316) paper by Doodlebug Design Inc

Page 36, Life Begins at 65 – life's journey domed goudy alphabet (557048) by K & Company, antique brass and antique silver charms by Scrapbooking Basics

Page 37, Creative Christening –funny decoration kit (baby boy & girl) by Make Me, vellum colour blocks (pastel) and vellum rainbow stickers by Mrs Grossman's Paper Company

Page 38 Ghouls' Night Out
Halloween haunted wood (JJ-1203) and fright night (JJ-1204) buttons by Craftime

Page 42, Easter Bunny – daisy die-cut alphabet stickers and daffodil flat paper (643077 637368) by K & Company

Page 42, Merci – jelly labels (thank you 2) by Making Memories

Page 43, Dashing Dad – Susan Winget green vines card (SL117SW), Susan Winget green fibre (SL111SW), pine (SL109SW) and cherry cobbler (SL107SW) papers by Paper Adventures, Labelz dad (04034), antique round copper brads (23742) and charmed phrases (fathers) by Making Memories

Page 43, Gone but not Forgotten – ladybug/candy apple megastrip (924) paper, ladybug posies (490) and tokens by Doodlebug Design Inc

Page 44, 21st Birthday – Bulk (5005-710) paper by Frances Meyer, snapshots soccer (38020) card stock stickers by Pebbles Inc.

Page 48, Wedded Bliss – Bordeaux floral (643077 639751) and Bordeaux stripe (643077 639805) papers and towering type cardstock alphabet stickers by K & Company

Page 49, Remember When – hippy chick flashy flowers (7-7207) paper, die-cut tags (7-7272) and tropical punch alphabet stickers (7-3902) by SEI

Page 50 You're One Today – Celery squares and celery dots card by Lasting Impressions, busy scrappers solution for girls to women pages (HOTP 3293) by Hot Off The Press

Page 54, A Great Grandpa – alpha-caps (LTT-667) by Lli'l Davis Designs, playtime mix (MX101BJ) paper pack by Paper Adventures

Page 55, Happy Mother's Day – paper by PSX

Page 56, Thank You – Alyssa Collection (BP-AP-AL02, BP-AP-AL03 & BP-AP-AL04) papers by Bella Press, senti-metals (SM106) by Lasting Impressions

Page 60 Santa's Little Helper – twinkly stripes (5301-092) paper by Frances Meyr Inc, seasons (23731) page Bubbles

Page 61 Birthday Keepsake – dark colour staples (22828) by Making Memories, kids 8 x 8in paper pack (HOTP 5202) and kids 8 x 8in cardstock pack (HOTP 5208) by Hot Off The Press

Page 62 It's a Boy! – Fundamentals bubble blue Os (877) paper by Doodlebug Design Inc, it's a boy (5306-108) paper by Frances Meyer Inc, simply stated Heidi rub-on alphabet by Making Memories, baby boy sayings rub-on transfers (RO-32) by Me and My BIG Ideas, sweetwater photo stickers (SW150) by Who, textured trios stylish brads by Queen & Co

Page 66, Forbidden Corner – tags and labels (ACS-026), confused (ACS-055) and pistachio (ACS-044) papers from the Aged & Confused Sublime Collection by Basic Grey, letter stickers (MOT-081) and clay (MOT-062) paper from Motifica Collection and embossed stickers by Basic Grey, jumbo slide mounts (HOTP7502) by Hot of the Press, clear memorabilia pockets by Xyron

Page 67, Open House – origins stipple (SL103OR), golden diamondback (SL100OR) and native quilt (SL106OR0 papers by Paper Adventures, alphabet tile embellishments by Make Me, twill stripes gathering place (EXPTS06) and mother of mine (EXPTS03) by All My Memories, Halo button snaps

Page 68, Birthday Surprise – Birthday border (643077 638914) and birthday lime texture (643077 638938) flat papers and stickers by K & Company

Page 72, You're Grand – crystal effects alphabet by Dovecraft

Page 73 Especially for you – holiday images (643077 637863), ornament border (643077 637894) and red patchwork (43077 637870) flat papers, holiday traditions die-cut alphabet stickers and holiday traditions embossed stickers by K & Company, letters (70-007) paper by Penny Black, bitty buckles (Heritage) by Jest Charming

Page 74, Sweet Sixteen – Pastel wild flowers paper (183), pastel taffy stripes (188) paper, shabby chick (648) repositionable alphabet stickers, pastel cardstock stickers (704) and pastel round sequins (1641) by Doodlebug Design Inc, love you photo anchor eyelets by Eyelet Outlet

Page 79, Across The Miles – Paper Pizazz vellum dots (35788 15511) by Hot Off The Press, oversized tags (23202) and simply stated rub-on Heidi alphabet by Making Memories, snowflakes by Crafty Bitz

Page 80, Friendship Album – Dictionary (643077 636279), postcard (643077 636262), flowers & letters flat papers, pansy 6 x 6in paper pad, LJ Letters printed embossed vellum, embossed stickers, Grand Adhesions (puzzle pieces), string clasp from the Life's Journey range by K & Company, photo anchors, mini circle brads and rub-ons (Expressions) by Making Memories, ABC skid stickers by Creative Imaginations

Page 86, Memory Album – Time & again (TA-P1 and TA-P2) paper collections by Déjà Views, heritage cardstock pack (HOTP 5207) by Hot Off the Press, photo flips (rectangle 23145), decorative brads (pewter round 23721), alphabet charms small circle (22656), ribbon charms (mr1 23184), charmed quotes (mother 23794), charmed plaques (nature 23492), charmed phrases (time 23780), charmed photo corners (hearts 22717), charmed flower (24785) by Making Memories, soft blue jean/soft swimming pool (981) and birthday boy striped paper (285) by Doodlebug Design Inc., white velveteen paper (sugar V500 SO) by Paper Adventures, snowflake buttons (think snow) by Buttons Galore, acrylic tags (clearly yours 557437) by K & Company, Crystal Stickers bubble alphabet (Style 1178 and 1171)

Page 92, Let's Ski Album – Soft blue jean/soft swimming pool (981) and birthday boy striped paper (285) by Doodlebug Design Inc., white velveteen paper (sugar V500 SO) by Paper Adventures, snowflake buttons (think snow) by Buttons Galore, acrylic tags (clearly yours 557437) by K & Company, Crystal Stickers bubble alphabet (style 1178 and 1171)

Suppliers

UK

Courtyard Crafts
Brimstage Hall, Brimstage,
Wirral CH63 6JA
tel: 0151 342 4216
www.courtyardcraft.co.uk
e-mail: sales@courtyardcraft.co.uk
Mail-order service available.
Scrapbooking papers, rubber
stamping products, peel-offs,
stickers, buttons, punches,
general craft tools and materials

Crab Apple Crafts
Georgian House, Lady Heyes Craft
Centre, Kingsley Road, Frodsham,
Cheshire WA6 6SU
tel: 01928 787 797
www.crabapplecrafts.co.uk
e-mail: rosemary@thescrapbookst
ore.co.uk
Scrapbooking papers, rubber
stamping products, peel-offs,
stickers, buttons, punches, general
craft tools and materials

Crimson Crafts
Red House Farm & Tea Rooms,
Red House Lane, Dunham
Massey, Cheshire WA6 6SU
tel: 0791 704 2782
www.crimsoncrafts.co.uk
Scrapbooking papers, rubber
stamping products, peel-offs,
stickers, buttons, punches, general
craft tools and materials

Esselte
Esselte UK Ltd.
Waterside house, Cowley
Business Park, High Street,
Cowley, Uxbridge, UB8 2HP
tel: 01895 878 700
www.esselte.co.uk
Dynamo and Xyron

Fotospeed
6b Park Lane Industrial Estate,
Park Lane, Corsham, Wilts,
SN13 9LG
tel: 01249 714333
www.fotospeed.com
Photo papers and deckle-edge
ruler

Hobbycraft
Visit the website or phone for
details of your nearest store
tel: 0800 0272387
www.hobbycraft.co.uk
Large variety of art and craft
materials

Ilford
Ilford Imaging UK Limited, Town
Lane, Mobberley, Knutsford
Cheshire WA16 7JL
tel: 01565 6843000
www.ilford.com
Photo papers

Letraset Ltd
Kingsnorth Industrial Estate,
Wotton Road, Ashford, Kent,
TN23 6FL
tel: 1233 624421
www.letraset.com
Studio Tac Adhesive

US

Ilford
Ilford Imaging USA Inc
West 115 Century Road
Paramus, NJ 07652
tel: 1-201-265-6000
Photo papers

Michaels
Michaels Stores Inc
8000 Bent Branch Drive
Irving
TX 75063
tel: 972 409 1300
www.michaels.com
Large variety of art and craft
materials

A. C. Moore
130 A.C. Moore Drive
Berlin
New Jersey 08009
tel: 856 228 6700
www.acmoore.com
Large variety of art and craft
materials

Jo-Ann
Visit the website or phone for
details of your nearest store
tel: 1 888 739 4120
www.joann.com
Large variety of art and craft
materials

Acknowledgments

Once again my family has given me so much love and unconditional support during the ups
and downs of writing a book. Ian, you are an incredible person and a stable rock in my dizzy
upside down creative world. Thank you just isn't enough.

Joshua and Sarah you are now growing so fast and I am so very proud to be your mum.
Thanks for indulging me and posing for photographs; life with you is never dull!

I would also like to thank the following:
• My brothers Christopher and Paul, their wives, Christine and Liza, my gorgeous niece
Millie and adorable nephew Leon, for all their interest and encouragement.
• Elsie and John who once again gave me tremendous support, particularly by taking their
grandchildren out twice a week during the summer of 2005 so that I could make up lost time.
• My good friends Val, Susan, Gill, Dianne and Charlotte. You are such amazing women and
just like sisters to me.
• My hand model Gill Williamson. Your positive and caring attitude once again made our
journeys to London good fun and virtually stress free.
• Karl Adamson who made all our photo sessions really enjoyable with his great humour and
artistic influence.
• Emma at Letraset, Louisa at Trim Craft and Paul at Esselette for their help with materials.
• All at David & Charles who have made this book a reality. Especially Cheryl Brown for
commissioning me before *Surprisingly Simple Novelty Cards* had even been printed and for
all her help and support during a very difficult time. Prudence Rogers and Jennifer Proverbs
for fitting so much into an amazing layout and design. And Betsy Hosegood, it was a real
pleasure to work with you once again.

About the author

Following on from
*Surprisingly Simple Novelty
Cards* this is Sue's second
book for David & Charles
Sue is a regular contributor
to several magazines
including *Making Cards,
Paper Inspirations* and
Practical Crafts magazines.
She lives in Cheshire,
England, with her husband, Ian, and two children.
Sue has her own website, www.suenicholson.com,
where there is a reader's gallery, tips, ideas and
links. She would love to hear from you so please
email her at noveltycards@suenicholson.com

Index